POEMS FAR & WIDE

Also by John Jenkins

POETRY

Growing up With Mr. Menzies (John Leonard Press, 2008); *Dark River* (Five Islands Press, 2003); *A Break in the Weather, a verse novel* (Modern Writing Press, 2003); *Days Like Air* (Modern Writing Press, 1992); *The Wild White Sea* (Little Esther, 1990); *Chromatic Cargoes* (Post Neo, 1986); *The Inland Sea* (Brunswick Hills, 1984); *Blind Spot* (Makar, 1977); *Zone of the White Wolf* (Contempa, 1974)

CO-WRITTEN, WITH KEN BOLTON

Lucky for Some (Little Esther, 2012); *Poems of Relative Unlikelihood* (Little Esther, 2005); *Nutters Without Fetters* (Press Press, 2002); *The Wallah Group* (Little Esther, 2001); *Gwendolyn Windswept, a verse novel* (serialized in *Otis Rush* Magazine, 1994); *The Gutman Variations* (Little Esther, 1993); *The Ferrara Poems, a verse novel* (Experimental Art Foundation, 1989); *Airborne Dogs and Other Collaborations* (Brunswick Hills, 1988)

PROSE FICTION

The Arthur Tantrum Letters, a fictional biography, with Robert Harris (Stitch and Time, 1975); Anthology: *The Outback Reader*, short fiction (co-ed., with Michael Dugan, Outback Press, 1974)

NON-FICTION

Anthology: *Travelers' Tales of Old Cuba* (ed., Ocean Press U.S.A., 2002, 2011, 2014, 2016); *Arias: Recent Australian Music Theatre* (co-author, with Rainer Linz, Red House Editions, 1997); *22 Australian Contemporary Composers* (co-author with others, New Music Articles, 1988)

ANTHOLOGY, AS ED.

Eclogues: Newcastle Poetry Prize Anthology 2007 (co-ed., with Jan Owen, Martin Harrison, Hunter Writers Centre, 2007); *Soft Lounges,* experimental writing (co-ed., with Antonia Bruns, Melbourne Fringe Festival, 1984); *Cherries and Quartermasters,* experimental writing (co-ed. with David Miller, Paper Castle, 1975)

THEATRE, RADIO PLAYS, LIBRETTO/MUSIC/SONGS, FILMSCRIPT, INSTALLATION

The Four (and a Half) Seasons, sampled natural sounds, electronically treated piano with fragments of sampled and treated recordings, John Jenkins website, 2018; *Homage,* mixed theatre performance, co-written and devised with berni janssen, Francesca Sasnaitis, Javant Biarujia (Jolt Performance Space, Melbourne, 2010); *Undue Voice: Tremor,* theatre/poetry co-written and devised with berni janssen, Emilie Collyer, Ian Irvine; with music by James Hullick and Daniel Beuss (Performance Space, Castlemaine, 2009); *Under The Shaded Blossom* (Radio play, ABC Radio National Airplay series, 2006); *Open Your Eyes, Exercise* (Radio play, co-written with Rainer Linz, Radio 3RRR, Melbourne, 1991); *Waiting for Manana*: John Jenkins, Kim Bessant & Friends, 4T Cassettes, 1991 (updated and republished as CD, *Walking Upright,* 2000); *The Ferrara Poems* (Film-script, co-written with Ken Bolton, directed by Jenni Robertson, 1990, Frames International Film Festival); *"Quotations",* installation, performance and video, with Tish Banks, Michele Luke, Charlie Rees, Jenni Robertson, Jyanni Steffensen, Mark Thompson, Curtis Weiss, Craig Tidswell (video by Shane Carn and Sunday Mission (Experimental Art Foundation, 1990)); *Play for Voices,* libretto, music composed by Richard Vella (Melbourne Astra Choir, 1981); *Arts Bounce Back,* theatre, co-written and performed with Kim Bessant, Margaret Norwood (La Mama Theatre, Melbourne,1978); *Dance Films,* theatre, co-written and devised with Lisa Roberts, Rosie Simons, Margaret Norwood, Kim Bessant (La Mama Theatre, Melbourne,1978); *Arthur Tantrum: A Fictional Biography, A Biographical Fiction* (installation and performance, co-written and devised with Robert Harris, Central Street Gallery, Sydney, 1977)

Poems Far & Wide

JOHN JENKINS

PUNCHER & WATTMANN

First published in 2019
Published by Puncher and Wattmann
PO Box 279
Waratah NSW 2298

http://www.puncherandwattmann.com
puncherandwattmann@bigpond.com

ISBN: 978-1-925780-12-3

A catalogue record for this book is available from the National Library Australia.

Cover design by Miranda Douglas
Text design by Christine Bruderlin
Printed by Lightning Source International

This project has been assisted by the Australian Government through the Australia Council, its arts funding and advisory body.

Contents

Minifesto

Dear Reader, be warned . . .
I think poetry is everywhere the poem goes,
the idea of a chosen plenitude: found in
hard-nosed science; in fantasy and dreams;
in satire, song, in wit and humour; drama high
and low. The list goes on: the simple and sublime,
serious or subtle, emotions fine and raw; in tradition
and the new; or words that seem to write themselves.
Equally in wonder, work and wishes; in reverie
while washing dishes, any human thing!

Something Pokes

(a poem bookmark)

Something pokes its head up
staking its claim in
the pages of a universe
we call *book*.

Off you go then, little
paper peg, leave a unique
trace from Abacas
to Zoology.

Hands may plant you,
then pull you out again,
and lines will
deepen in those hands.

As text speaks our true
minds into being –
balanced too on spines
as readers are.

Slim surveyor,
remind me where I'm up to,
and help unfold
a dog-eared hour.

Say *"here is where
you left off reading"*
turn each page
on whisper wings
and fly!

Dandelion Seeds

launching pads on thin dry stalks
pin-cushions stuck with parachutes you blow
white tears the wind lifts, trailing swollen seeds

air filters out each fine thread, web-like dancings,
white tears, tiny silver flames
on silken dreams of summer's wind-fall

then another wheel of radiant spokes
floats like sudden upward-drifting snow

each loose-leaf swollen shiver-sphere
explodes its airy froth of stars

I drift with them to barely skim the breeze
to live or fall beyond this page . . .

A Year of Blue Moons

Gone Troppo Postcard

– for M. C.

Dear Big Mort –
I'm sitting in the Shell Bar today
drinking rum and coconut 'sunbeams'
through a long glass straw
watching the palms 'lean and lilt'
in fragrant trade-winds
as the sky above the reef just smoulders
into red and orange sunset.

I've thrown away my watch, passport, iPad
and identity, and have learned to sleep
standing up (still clutching sunbeams in my hand).
Daily, I wear the entire beach
as my sandshoes and spend more 'quality time'
with the nice tourist girls, riding turtles in the surf.
They seem to think I'm over-dressed, so I've swapped
my white-tie suit for a cool, loose *lavalava* of banana leaves.

If I ever leave this place, I'll see you
back in Melbourne . . .

That is, if you're not yourself
already smiling down,
a kindly portrait from some
postage stamp in Trinidad.
                    – Cheers, JJ

Under the Shaded Blossom

The poet Wallace Stevens (1879–1955) worked life-long
as an insurance executive. He first visited Cuba in 1923.
Meyer Lansky (1902–1983) was the Mafia's
chief deal-maker and strategist in Havana after 1930.
The best and the worst: the poem imagines them
meeting in 'the Jewel of the Antilles'.

Into Havana's noonday glare, Meyer Lansky slips
from the shadowy front of the *Compañía Hotelera*
La Riviera de Cuba. Jumpy at dislocating knee-cymbal crashes
of a passing beggar band. But ol' cool eyes doesn't sweat
so quick – bent brim of a pork-pie hat, and tie so thin it's just
one strand of discreet silk. He's absorbing rays on the
stone steps, abstracted for a while, figuring the numbers.
"When I got to the room and the bellhop flicked back them
big curtains! Boy! I could see almost the whole city.
Like it was in my hand. It was the palm trees that got me first.
Every place you see, there was palm trees. It made me feel like
I was back in Miami in the good old days, with Lucky
and them guys. Everything is *here!*" – he taps brim
for luck and turns the felt down. "All in my head.
(Don't never take notes, don't write nothing down.)
No one comes breathing down your neck here.
And only ninety miles from the coast.
Practically America, it is!" A quick flick
of his tongue, and Lansky skips out into space opening
up around him; the swinging door of a cream Chevrolet,
as the air closes around any trace of *the gringo financier* . . .
Tonight, he'll hit the Hotel Sevilla Biltmore, the Gran,
the Summer, Chateau Madrid, the dazzling Sans Souci,
La Concha, spin the wheels, catch the acts, and collect-up big.
He has just signed the Cuban American Realty Company.

"Even sounds legit! When me and Lucky first talked about buying
into real estate, them wise guys thought that we was nuts.
Them guys couldn't see beyond their bowls of spaghetti!"

A canary in a cage might seem less free in the morning, though
it sweeten a balcony with song. Mr. Stevens looked up
to it, and the white tuft of hair above the broad forehead
also tilted, and a tie was loosed slightly from its pin.
Mr. Stevens – Vice President of a prudential company –
today thought the air almost as elemental as the sea,
invisible colours no less vibrant than sun-drenched ones.
Here, time would reveal a succession of facades, each imagined
from pink stone, born of light, atmosphere and sea gloss. It was
close and brisk (he meant the Malecón) where he strolled and held
upright his parasol and thoughtful face, which held its own
deep quietness, and every shade of light and shade of song. Mr. Stevens,
elaborating a palette both abstract and precise, recalled at once the rail
journey down Florida. How Havana always welcomed his
appraisal, how real things revealed themselves to him,
they changed to music, passing an old casino in the park, where the bills
of swans had lowered slowly as he had neared. *"For him?"* In this way,
    life gave
its assurance to always change, that something new and shining
    would appear,
arising anew from its patina. *("Husks, wherein time was cradled.")*
The stone (he noted now) became rose, and clouds like lightest rose
at evening. And here, too, a single quiet dwelt, within poems made
    of things;
or orchestras played, balloons lifted into tropical nights at festivals
    he meant

also to attend. (He was a life-lover, after all.) The Malecón stirred with extrinsic music, as did the sea. He watched it lift, through its filigreed notation, leaning into the sea wind with a pencil, and wrote now for an hour, the brine wind turning him neat and leather-bound. Good, Mr. Stevens. Stare out the cannon placements on the distant Moro! They once stared down pirates, protected treasure galleons in Havana Bay. Here Columbus, that thief of blood and gold, found a sea road back to Spain. He founded empires.

Mr. Stevens, as he did every morning, awoke at six
then read for two hours in his balcony room, becoming
furious at the British *New Statesman,* brought with him
from Hartford, its pungent anti-Americanism, with which
he only part agreed; then the latest on Garbo, his favourite
star. (He dreamed a meeting with her.) Put down the rag,
to then re-read *The Tempest* ('wond'rous play') as always,
ritualistically, on all his first mornings in Havana. The coffee
by his elbow drifted a delicious lick of steam, into old tracery
of leaves wrought in iron above the wakening street.
His breakfast pleased him: a sweet bean confection. "Yep
it was," with milk curd. "Memo: Ship a packet back to Hartford."
Especially, he enjoyed the sky, the moist climate of
red flowers and tropical sensuality. And the air. Brine-
scented, special isle. Something soft and sweet about the
air alright, all the way down from Florida, peachy cream on skin,
free champagne, and your senses 'inside-out': all around
you, in bright lights, and waiting to be let back in. *"Ha! A neat
conceit, brother!"* He read on: *"Methought the billows spoke
and told me of it . . . The wind did sing it to me . . ."*

Meyer drank in silence, pernod, for the *woims,* in the early morning hours, with the window of his room open. The Hotel Sevilla Biltmore was built at a cost of 2.5 million pesos, in American gold. Meyer, who'd fixed it all up – *"Nine casinos and six hotels now!"* – preferred the Hotel Nacional, just like Big Lucky. The old-style charm and luxury, tempered by good taste. *"Convenient too for meets – a salon for Batista's stooges, and private elevator with gilded ironwork for my tame 'El Presidente'."* Meyer was pensive, dressed in his underwear. He liked to bathe at sunrise, move at random 'bout the room in the first cool air, sprinkle on talcum powder, before sitting on that little balcony. It was either pernod or milk, nothing else. An occasional dame from one of Marina's houses. But he liked to keep his pecker clean. His wife back in the States: *"Two daughters! And no nose powder."* He liked to keep his wig straight, too. *"All that crap was for the suckers . . . Funny, how you can have everything . . ."* yet the thing that delighted him most was the noise of the waves at night. The pernod looked faintly blue, in this light. Maybe he was getting soft. Later, he would have his driver stop the car near the old monument to the U.S.S. Maine, and walk around a bit and think. Mostly, he just liked to think. *"The four New York families wanted in, but me and Lucky keeps them schmucks out!"* An austere life. *"You go unnoticed. Don't make waves, just make bucks. An' you make sure everyone in your operation behaves."* It was just business. *"Sure!"* Near the monument, he could walk and think. Away from all the noise and glitz, the overheated deals and the little wooden balls in the rigged roulette wheels, in the biggest cat house in the Caribbean. Breathe sea air without saying a word to no-one. *"All that fresh salt air."* Or the scenery near *Quinta Avenida* (Fifth Avenue) was pretty. *"A surprise visit maybe . . . that barber shop, where*

the New York capos hang out Sundays. Short back and insides,
all round! Schmucks is right! But think it all out first, maybe . . ."

A big blue bow seemed drawn down to join, *sans* any
seeming, a more cobalt sea, where the earth curved away
under blue-flake sky, as Mr. Stevens discreetly departed
Marina's. "*The music crept by me upon the waters*
with its sweet air, thence I have followed it." Still,
picturing somehow an indolent progression of swans,
strolled past a toothless grandmother with a
basketful of pears for sale. Sadly, an old wall had
absorbed the heat of the sun, and limp leaves fell.
He reached up to a flower – "*To touch again the hottest*
bloom might become, what?" – and chuckled. When
writing, he liked to travel alone. Packages of various
gourmet foods were already mailed home. Even from
here, he could turn the keys to Florida, unlock with cash
his cosmopolitan yearnings. He was tall, austere, dignified,
an unusual looking man. This day he wore a wide-brimmed
Panama, having shed his pinstripes for a light, white
suit of cotton. And he loved to walk. He'd just walk round
by himself, anywhere. A slow stride, peered deliberately
from beneath his brim, peered at everything, intently.
There were shops, there were streets, old lanes
and ancient shade trees. There was always
this and that. There were antique Spanish lamps to
collect for a polished table back in Hartford.
They revolved, lamp and table, in his mind. He knew
the shop was somewhere by, close to his embassy,
near the old monument to the U.S.S. Maine – "*Remember*

the Maine!" had inflamed gimcrack populists and tub-
thumping senators, jingoistic freebooters with their eyes
on the biggest fruit dish in the *Antilles* – Mr. Stevens reflected.
Then, turning near the statue, an odd-looking little guy shoved
past neatly, without looking up and muttering. Stevens saw:
"Porkpie hat, face like a cod – dead cold eyes –
or maybe more reptilian. Black Italian suit!" and, to his ear,
New York corners in the voice – *" Touch of Jewish, Polish,*
maybe Sicilian? Did he really say that: *'I'll fix the schmuck'?"*

Lunch was not in the least a complete fiasco. The genius
(the spirit) of this island must be a chef; the dishes
capturing a mind at play, in the cuisine sense.
Lists of ingredients were displayed on a white card
menu, a stellar bill of fare: *"Black beans, rice a la marinera,*
Creole salads; avocado, pineapple and juicy cuts of roast
pork; crab and queenconch enchiladas from the southern
archipelago. Roast breast of flamingo, tortoise stew,
roast tortoise with lemon and garlic, crayfish from
Cojímar, oysters from Sagua, and grilled swordfish;
venison chops from Camagüey, the succulent mystery of
the manatee. " Quiet corner, old oak table, amidst the napery
and silver setting. He ate alone. He was alone. He chose
small portions of several dishes, without haste or greed.
He savoured a tropic inventiveness. And sent a message with the waiter,
back to the chef: a tip for white hats. *" Well done amigo!"*
A poet can be gourmet, and executive. Worlds widen
to allow, like a girth let out on holiday, that living should
be lived, enjoyed, an adventure. Here's nice logic for
the prim: *"Appetites are part of nature and, as part of nature,*

13

part of us." The waiter bought over a message on a tray.
From the smiling cod man at the bar. "*Pork-pie hat!*"
Mr. Stevens saw *him* again – tap his brim when he
looked up. "*Invitation to share a drink. Odd. There was something –
more than – peremptory about it. A message from a boss.*"
Threw the card back on the tray, and made his way across.

Lansky met him at the big doorway of the grand casino
of the Hotel Nacional's dining room. The two men
shook hands, and the taller was ushered to the bar,
just in sight of the green-felt tables where louche cards
skimmed and fell. "Mr. Stevens, Meyer Lansky. How
was your meal, Pal?" "Excellent. How do you know
my name? Are you the manager?" "Let's say, I have an
interest. We like our friends to have a good time here –
I take care of people in Havana. Yeh, Pal. Especially with the quality,
business people from the States. The meal's on me!
Now, let me buy you a drink – and some chips. Black-
jack or craps?" "Thank you, but I don't gamble."
"Sure, Pal. Forget the craps. Maybe later. Let's have a drink
and talk. What's your poison? Aged rum, Hatuey beer,
Montecristo cigar? Myself, I drink milk, or pernod – pernod,
for the *woims.*" Lansky patted his waist . . . "You can't be
too careful." (*The guy's a chump*, thought Lansky. *Coulda
turned free chips into notes – just one spin of the wheel.
And if he blew 'em, no loss. Then cut out.*) Mr. Stevens
sipped his seven-year-old rum. It was honey and fire, burnt
honey and smoke. (*Touch of heaven, touch of hell here –
and fortunes rising, sinking on a whirl. This Mr. Lansky
is spruiking for that sweet, ruinous addiction.*) "Tell

me, Mr. Stevens, what's your game? You do back in the States?"
"Well, I'm Vice President of the Hartford
Accident and Indemnity Insurance Company. Formerly
Of the New York Office of the Equitable Surety Co.
of Saint Louis." "Insurance, heh Pal?
Well, lotsa people have accidents. Tell you, here I'm
thinking of something big. To roll some big cigars.
Banks, insurance, hotels, airfields – *to bring lotsa stuff
across* – imports, exports. Our peanut people – I mean,
the gold-braid flunkeys – will help the moves. Heard of
the Compañía Hotelera La Riviera de Cuba? Nope.
Well, fine. Here's my card. Maybe we could do a deal."
"What sort of deal?" (Mr. Stevens thought, *The world
suddenly a bauble for agents of a suspect generosity.
What sort of instant business this? It has an odour.
This is some 'monster of the isle, many legs and hands'.*)
"Tell me, Mr. Stevens, can I be straight?" "Please do so, sir,
you have my word it will go no further. My discretion is
absolute." (*You bet, it is. You bet it won't!* Lansky smiles.)
"We're looking for a legit firm for some
tricky mainland deals. What we do and the books
don't need any hard looking at, you understand. Things
sorta go round in slow circles. It ain't so obvious. There's
a code, and lots of just knowing what to do, without
saying much. What you get is paid cash, Pal, a river of cash,
to buy up real estate, and lots of gilt policies in case things
fall flat. That's the deal. I don't want to say no more for now.

"What say?" (*Maybe a photograph next time at Marina's,
if the chump says no,* thought Lansky. *Shoulda already*

done that. Shoulda thought of that, already.) Mr. Stevens
sighed. *(This is a dangerous place. Be careful. He clearly
governs this tin heaven. The first act, his gladhand bribe,
the next – entrapment. So, the earth's 'alive with creeping men'.
So, 'mechanical beetles never quite warm'. His gilt-edge
like poison, 'given to work a great time after'.)* "Mr. Lansky,
I thank you for your hospitality. And for your interest in our firm.
I studied Law at Harvard, and graduated from law school
in New York in 1903. I was admitted to the bar a year later.
Let me tell you, I have so constituted our company, that all our books
are watched by many eyes, and from all sides, all ferociously
legal. To have any dealings with me would place your affairs
under a scrutiny most intense, purely as a matter of course.
But so you don't feel chipped, let me buy *you* a drink now –
a pernod, for the *woims!*" Lansky slapped his new pal
on the back. "Sure Pal, sure. So, forget it. Enjoy your stay
on old Havana. Tell your friends. As I said, we just like
everyone to have a good time. No hard feelings. Sure! In fact,
I made the whole pot up. I aint got no companies. I wuz only
raising you, to see your hand. I don't want no crooks
or takers hanging round my casino. Not with all this
moolah in the air. Hey, you did right. You got a flush there,
Pal. You played it! It's refreshing to meet an honest
man in Cuba. Like fresh air. I mean it! As I said, I just
handle security. You can't be too careful, *Pal.*"

Mr. Stevens thought, "*There are two classes of people –
those who bother you with letters, and those that do
not.*" He preferred postcards, and shot off fair fleets of
them, each as brief and perfect as a sonnet. Smoke signals

16

without pain, and stamps as pretty as the pictures, too.
He sent them from the good heart of America, from an
impulse, from Jefferson to Lincoln, and from the ones who
send her hope: the darker heart eclipsed for now, a hood-
ed chandelier, closed cantina, in full tropic sun, which lit
new paths to wander, into the old town, *Habana Vieja*.
He looked at the stones, melting now beneath his feet.
"Away they shine there! *In the acute intelligence of their
own imagination*. Imagination, don't let us down. Be your best,
your promise. *As if we spoke of light itself, of objects
and light. So, too, the mind adds nothing new – it adds
nothing, except itself..*" He saw an endless procession
of new faces and, beneath every foot, a stone melting,
and every stone a moment coming, and from the sea
in new freshness and glosses, anointed with salt water.
He drank the air before him, as if all that was old was new
again, and some were a poetry, all taking delight in its own
making lavish – as if of that *might be* it was truly made.

Miracle on Blue Mouse Street, Dublin

For Leo Cullen who said: "Once
Celtic Tiger Ireland; now no teeth!"

"Miracles For Sale! Compact and Portable!"
In a doorway from the rain, on Blue Mouse Street,
he was shouting "Miracles! More miracles to come!"
The old beggar with the battered suitcase said,
"Yes, I am sure there will be one for you."

He spoke conspiratorially when he saw my coins.
"Come closer," he said. "To me, you look
a little worried, as if lacking air, or *joie de vivre*;
but are lucky anyway. Because I see my suitcase
is going to open for you, and I believe a miracle
might well appear. And I look forward to knowing
how this suitcase miracle will manifest itself,
as I am now quite certain that it will!

"Now listen," he said, and don't miss out."
He took a plastic comb, held it to his mouth
and hummed and wheezed dreadfully through it.
"That tune is called 'Our Happiness'," he said.
It made all the sparrows shake up from the trees.
And made small children run and cry, and the rain fall much harder.
He smiled, twirled and did a little hop and broken dance.

"I love my life," he said. "I love selling hope and miracles
out here in the rain, to all the passers-by on Blue Mouse Street.
Look," he said, "I have a pocket full of holes.
These are my 'loopholes', and I pay no tax."
And he pulled all his pockets inside out, and showed me.
"I had a pocket full of hope once, but hope or fine illusions,

18

or any sort of negotiable miracle, all being invisible,
weigh less than a suitcase I carry for a rainy day like this one,
always hoping for a miracle to manifest, for my paying public.

"Look!" And I imagined I saw us both standing there,
just then, and something was moving. "Yes, I believe
it is already starting to manifest, or snap open," he said.
And the lid swung up and, inside his case,
I saw an old beggar open a suitcase. And inside that
was a smaller case, and us both standing there, leaning
over a case that had just popped open, and so on . . .
but when I turned, he was gone, and so was the suitcase.
Only a muddy puddle where he had stood, but I could still
hear his tune 'Our Happiness' wheezing faintly through the rain.

Puissance: *Marble Frieze, Parthenon, Athens*

For Olympic equestrian,
Dr. Reiner Klimke (1936–1999)

Etched now, in highest elevation above
a Doric column, the timeless frieze unfrozen:
un-stamped from her chaste stone, silent Athena
animates this stillness and breathe it into being.

Imagine every flank in motion, wide eyes and nostrils flaring,
hear the precise thud of hooves down centuries, Olympics.

To prance with delight and precision, the beast's mind
is still keen, still fresh; tamed with force unforced.
Unbroken spirits nod in proud agreement.

Of grace and beauty in classic riding, Xenophon wrote
in his Art of Equitation, *De Equis Alendis:* "What we need
is the horse should of his seeming own accord exhibit
all those finest airs without restraint, or least duress . . . "

The *Hohe Schule*, and liquid-maned 'Wind Horse'
of *haute école cheval*, white fire etched in alabaster,
the ease of collected lightning: strength defined and willingly
contained by reins, thunder held discreetly in reserve,
pure cadence of outline, soft, pliant and balletic.
Equus dance of gold-eyed stallions still entire,
bascule in liquid arabesque, high noble nose
in vertical salute, all in motion flows *sans* effort.
The neck is arched, never cruelly over-bent. Each stroke
of the sculptor's chisel transfers its liquid trance of light,
the proportion of all parts completes a muscular strength
held in, held back, contained in the perfect 'third position',

so too *piaffe, capriole, courbette, Airs Above the Ground* . . .
Cloud-maned *Sturm-pferde* pirouettes its sky-born reign.

Just as a lyre resonates, each string finely tuned, silent music
guides the rider's hands and torso, refined to a merest shift
of weight. This impulse engraved in classic light. Each line
sings with subtle listening, as polished volumes flow
into a solemn quiet. Steely poise of steeds, their balanced
might floating in serene self-carriage, graces cloudy golden
ratios of sky in dawn of light, high-dancing.

Noble eyes that flash with fire might flash
again to leap entablature or column!

View from a Red Pagoda

Shanghai, 1985
I arrived by ferry from Osaka, one of the first backpackers
from the West, confronted by a casual red-star suit. An acrid cigarette
hung over my passport; stamped off-hand, as guards waved me down
a ramp of bending planks. '*Capitalist Roader*' Deng Xiaoping
still in charge back then: 'The Little Bottle' bobbing up from the party's
many plots to sink him. At the close of Deng's first 10-year plan,
the 'Four Modernizations' dipped China's toe in The Tourism Sea
(though Deng blotted his name forever at Tiananmen in '89).
I can still feel that cold wind sweeping everyone along back then,
carrying rain over intricate webs of streets behind the Huanpu,
'river' in name only, more a clogged canal; its glorious DIY
of boats and motors cobbled from anything that might float
or putter: old timbers oiled for centuries, rafts pedal-powered,
poled or rowed. Above it all, The Bund an old Chicago-Style
high-rise elevation, of faded European Trade Concessions.
Scores of bicycles swarmed abreast down Nanjing Road, a thousand
bells warning! Everyone wore blue pyjamas, yawning out
of their 100-year dragon's sleep. I was their funny 'dancing
bear' back then on Renmin Street: when small huddles of the
curious gathered, to see a *long-nosed Round-Eye* (foreigner).
I lost myself back then, wandering in gloriously grubby
dragon-tiled lanes behind the intestinal Yu Gardens. Dumplings
steamed by the roadside, plum pastry for the cold. As shopkeepers
rattled cash tins, kitchens smoked with fat, while skinny babies
splashed in battered washing tubs in the middle of the street. I dossed
at the Peace Hotel, in makeshift dorms with unwashed sheets:
its precious antique furniture still under wraps and tarps. Now
touted as sheer upmarket deco luxury, with a conference hub.

Beijing, Shanghai, 2005
Mr Chen welcomes me to the Chinese Writers Centre in Beijing,
boasting how a new city the size of Canberra is being built in China
every month. Streets leap the new century, expanding all around me.
High fashion and pet dogs clash with old ways beneath overnight
crane and rubble sites. 'Little Emperors', pre relaxed one-child policy,
reign from silken prams. Flash cars and neon splutter in the people's
giant wok. Then I fly down south, where a fish-eye lens has magnified
Shanghai. The river-scape and skyline almost a futuristic touch-screen.
Joint-ventures in the air; brief-cased Westerners everywhere,
but people still businesslike and brisk. Everything *'shuangli'*,
as the saying goes, *direct and pleasantly sharp, like the autumn wind!*
To be polished by use, like an old key! Work hard, for the family!

Souzhou, 1985
Called 'the Venice of the East', this canal and garden city
remains a wonder of the world. Back then, my rip-off ticket was gouged
from a dapper station tout, but I jumped a two-hour queue.
He spoke English, a semi-legal 'guide', his earnings spent on prostitutes:
"No money no honey!" he explained, wrangling *renminbi* notes.
(A taste of things to come in Big Mac Beijing?) On the train, classical
Western music played: more nods and smiles when a chatty mother
who spoke only Mandarin recruited commuters to mind her
        things, while
she retrieved black kettles from a train guard; pouring tea for
the whole compartment. (Her practical humanity survives, I hope!)
In Souzhou, I discovered antique puzzle-gardens, which spiralled
intricately back upon themselves. I sipped in yum-cha tea rooms,
crossed delicate bridges over endless lattice-work canals.
Distantly, a huge steam train was still a willing work horse.

I walked and wondered. Finally, I climbed an ancient red pagoda: the view atop cloud-heady with the Way of Heaven, and recalled a poem by the wandering Tang vagrant, Meng Jiao: *"Such times! The traveller's heart is a flag – a hundred feet high in the wind!"*

Henri Matisse, Spring Studio, Nice

'Reclining Nude. The Painter and his Model 1935'

Luxe
His new odalisque refined as air and unadorned,
outlined like spectral light outstretched on canvas primed
with china gesso, still invisible to colour and to form . . .
He can almost feel her smile spreading warm as cat fur,
her eyes awaken to his hand. Morning sun throws barred shadows
where his pet doves coo: sea air, an arabesque of breath,
soft light of *la Belle Nice* pours into the casement studio.
He coaxes an almost transparent sable tip along the classic
shoulder. And life returns, enough for her to shrug or settle back:
as one arm ripples into sinuous swan's neck, precise glance
of pencil feathered from his wilder rainbow palette.

Calme
Henri's dressing gown trails across a morning's own chance pools
of reverie, he dusts charcoal across the delicious rumple of her couch,
as line of cheek turns gently and she faces us, her ideal viewer.
Her skin is soft as milk or velvet: all the heaven
he can wish on Earth, though Henri devoutly burns
a candle for the town's Madonna each Sunday in a fragrant chapel
by the beach. He prinks her counterpane with broken rosaries
of flowers, with stars of circus happiness, dancing diamonds
of delight, inking shells of almost blue, before returning to her eyes,
which stun him with the careless nonchalance of recognition.

Volupté
And dips again in kohl that swallows colour up, he mixes
with a little silken shade of whiter pulse: his entire being
and hers now hang on threads. He hesitates: What next?
Precision so attuned to sensual elegance, one upward curving lip

is perfect – classic nudity shivered into careful disarray, breast
fondly tipping to one side: he hears the sigh, but is it his?
Her womanly magnificence, after all, is natural grace emerged
from sleep. A silver necklet pulses on her throat, her lucent thigh
his stroke completes so tenderly, as though a line had drawn itself.
*

Finally, and daring all, he includes himself within the frame,
pen poised in foreground, and on the wall behind her couch
a looking glass, his eyes reflected, anticipates how any stranger
reads this poem; viewer and sheer act of viewing in a single glance.
And steps away to Amélie, now bathed in golden light.

Burnt Wood, Birch Bark and the Village of Creation

(Seven nested tales, in the manner of Matryoshka dolls)

*

Matryoshka's
heavy axe casts shadows in the dawning light.
The hardy woman of the forest strikes with all her might,
as chips fly round her apron. She gathers up split logs of birch.
The nights are cold, she thinks of her old *Babushka*,
how they sit together, dreaming by the winter fire.
Yes, she sees *Babushka* now, knitting that lovely
crimson shawl, its dancing weave of stories.

*

Babushka
looks up from her work. It will be a cosy
Nolinsk stole, to keep *Matryoshka's* shoulders warm.
A pot sits on the fire, bubbling now with bacon bones
and wild mushroom soup. *Babushka* smiles while counting out
more finished lines. Steam rising from the pot is like a wedding
veil. *Babushka* teases out new strands, red as cockerel combs,
traces her new tale, about that woman named *Alenka* –
there she is, *Alenka!* Who sings and
dances at the country fair.

*

Alenka, yes!
is singing of that foolish golden cockerel
whose crowing woke the sun. *Alenka's* lovely song fills
the Village of Creation with its light. The girl twirls now, in her
best *sarafan*, with its golden fringe, and joins the country dance.
"Please, *Alenka,* sing again," all beg of her, and so she does.
This time of a bride-to-be called *Katysha,*
who hastens in a cart to her wedding day in Moskva.

*

A wagon
carries *Katysha* past the morning fields:
her skirt is blue and burning cheeks are crimson.
Her mother whispered when she left: "You must come out
of your shell, and reveal the beautiful rose you are inside!
My *Katysha*, you will be a joyful bride!" As *Katysha* bumps along,
the morning mist dissolves in sun, just as she re-tells
an even older tale, about an enchanted Queen, *Shemakha,*
who defied a bad magician and turned into a star.

*

This is
the tale *Katysha*
tells herself, as fields of mist roll past:
Long ago, *Shemakha* was the brightest morning star,
one lustrous with new hope, after she outwitted bold Vladimir,
a sorcerer who stole her crown. From on high, *Shemakha* watches over
all of *Russkaja*, vowing one day to return to earth, but only when the time
is right. On that morning, full of light, Queen *Shemakha* will reclaim
her reign, taking care to work her ruler's art, while
disguised as a hardy woman of the forest.
See – all the mists of morning clear, as
she blazes down again!

*

Winter mist
rising, as old *Babushka* stirs
her mushroom soup, tale after tale unfolding in her mind:
So *Matryoshka* swings her axe forever, with buttery chips of birch
floating high, just as *Shemakha* flies down from the sky, and stands
beside that strong peasant woman of the woods. Miraculously,
they merge! Now time has come to thread fresh hope,
to paint new joy! With her return, *Shemakha*
cuts the tyrant's curse, and Vladimir
is banished.

*

Old *Russkaja*
breathes a sigh! Two wooden needles click
before a winter fire, as scent of birch bark and burnt wood
rises from the Village of Creation. Here each figurine is freshly made,
painted orange, gold and blue. Their open eyes look out at you,
and bright lips tell their tale. An orange blush deepens on each cheek,
and one becomes the next, as more red aprons dance,
unfolding generations. Each holds the centre of a poem,
held in turning hands upon this simple lathe.

**

Into
Matryoshka fits
Babushka; then *Alenka* in
her dancing *sarafan;* next *Katysha* with
her burning cheeks; as Queen *Shemakha*
appears a simple woman of the forest in her
pretty apron, and becomes *Matryoshka*
then back again, as each fresh and
painted face unfolds again
into itself as one.

***

Vietnam Postcards, Return to Saigon

2006: Pot, tripod, hearth and carp
The Kinh Vietnamese minority village in Thanh Hoa maintains
kitchen gods (small effigies) they believe will 'live' (or devoutly serve)
this blackened fireplace tripod. Dancing forever on the 23rd day
of the lunar calendar, these little godlings are 'invited' (taken out)
of the hearth, and ritually 'sent' on an annual quest, flashing off
into a beautiful dream realm, mounted on giant golden carp,
the same heroic deities you see in Vietnamese water puppetry –
brightly scaled and laughing fish, returned to nearby lakes
and rivers on their journey to Heaven! The villagers understand,
deep from their animist past, how timeless cultural memory
can refresh seasons, harvests, aquaculture, for essential survival.
The otherworldly is made practical, when those same carp are later
'invited' (cooked) to entertain the family around the same august
blackened pot, with their boiled tangy flesh now centrepiece
of favourite recipes, garnished with herbs and crunchy leaves.
As in legend, more than enough to swim around. To go around.

Garong, Chaum village
Unlock the *Garong*, a proud trunk for family treasure,
with three compartments. The middle one for silk, worn
on special days. The next stores gold, stones, jewellery,
legal documents of wealth, and funeral clothes. A *Klong*
contains pale bones, ancestral foreheads of the family dead.
The treasure trunk is fixed securely by the entrance door,
opened on carefully chosen lucky days. In an opium haze,
Baudelaire told of a lock of hair in one, years before
French Indo-China's vast colonial rule expired, finally, in 1954.

31

Weaving earth to sky
'Truth Beneficence Beauty Company Handicapped Handicrafts
Warehouse': by deft stump-treadle action they shuttle frail 'boats'
of silk, treading all day from East to West; thread West to East
and back again. Some amputees were children dodging US
    'carpet bombs'
in 'the American War'. Many hoed up waiting land mines; often babies
when they lost their limbs, now offer artisan refinements to a
    tourist bus.
"We specialize in lacquered wood, silk picture, lovely souvenir,
to help and prosper," says a smiley guide. Their hard survival,
as we straggle back, with our bubble-wrapped gifts from Nha Trang.

2015: Return to Saigon
On rails south, to Ho Chi Minh City
a speaker crackles its wonderful garbled English as I slow-train
endless outskirts and giant signage of . . . *Goodbye Hanoi
and your history attractions of sunset legend, your foods will live
in our hearts, listed by UNESCO as our new city of peace.*
And in my Saigon hotel, when I arrive, another sign
behind the door: *Please do not bring in room any weapon,
toxic product, atomic explosive, inflammable or pet animal.
Hotel not responsible of guests dying in rooms
from all previous drugs.* Very baffling, because this 'boutique'
hotel is brand new, in the centre of Saigon, with bustling
business conference rooms upstairs, ground-floor dining
hall replete with flowery urns. Wry-faced Taoist Immortals
ride oxen over lacquer panels; the foyer's Jade Emperor statue,
'Heavenly Grandfather', who calms all strife. So, who are
    these nightmare

signs meant for? There are no drugged-out conscripts here. Only hungry
guests, tables of brisk chatter, smiling local families, new vendors
and spenders from China, France and South Korea. Dishes whisked
from steaming self-serve tureens, all *ăn ngon miệng*, delicious!

Happy New Year! Everyone smiles, *Chúc Mừng Năm Mới!*
At breakfast, wishing a happy lunar reign of the monkey.
This thought-bubble pops a digital haze of flicker and buzz
as I wake from 31 satellite channels and cool hotel screen.
In the hall, a large tile portrait of Ho Chi Minh,
while the city that now bears his name, the 'old forest city'
of Saigon, rides a new tiger south from the Chinese border,
while trading with the USA: old tradition here,
of making former foes your new allies, after millennia
of Indo-Chinese wars with near neighbours you must still
live with, somehow. So enemy now friend, as rivers of people
at street level till out their mercantile selves,
the new energy transformative and giddy, as I watch
a young mother with two kids tucked behind swerve out
on her scooter, median age just 30, and getting younger every day.
The energy released seems delirious; roaring exhaust fumes
and noise. Everyone doing deals as I go down to the street.

Saigon Traffic. Here, stop dead! There are no lights, no crossings,
nothing. If you care about your life, you pause, and advance only
with infinite care. If this was the West, would they still give way
to timid flesh, in the absence of all rules? But the traffic slows,
socially attuned: drivers oddly sensitive among the swirling chaos
they create, though still ignoring 'One-Way' signs. The modern temper
of this broiling mass remains group-minded, the civilization deep.

So *mot, hai, ba, YOOOO!* (One, two, three, CHEERS!) I take
my heart in hand, and slowly cross the street:
look left, look right again, wade in slow motion, a river bent
with traffic – and somehow survive!

Di Nao! Let's Go! First, tread Shoe Street; then another
spruiking engine parts where a score of avenues branch off,
each one selling separate wares. On one long stretch
of dental-tourism clinics, windows grin white teeth
and lucky money frogs bite bright coins. 'We must feed
our family' is understood by all. But here that family
extends like arms of the mighty Mekong, fingering new tributaries
down generations of ever-branching marriage ties, into a living
Delta; *90 million at last count.* Many still sleep in heaped-up
doorways, then wheel out daily trolleys, fix punctures,
hawk peeled fruit. But fewer beggars here than last time.
The mood full swing, a new dawn popping fast.
The Party will fix the snarls, snags, pollution, and glaring ills
of State Capitalism later. Or not. Meanwhile, *Cham phan cham!*
(*bottoms up!*) Get rich, First World, a better life!

The Traveller (Man with a Suitcase)

After 'The Traveller 1973', by Jeffrey Smart (1921–2013)
in Queensland Art Gallery collection

Here he is again, that man with a suitcase, always stepping
from another bus, his reflections reflected everywhere,
in every other. He is always leaving distant towns, always
arriving, where aircraft blink and tow their delayed wish and rumble.
Too well-travelled for any traces of regret, he has rarely ceased
to love or properly care. His itinerary, and not least his mind, claims
each new sunny day, along with tomorrow's weeping rain; new morning
fog seeping through wire fences at the outskirts. Nor does he despair
when his identity is more akin to silence; on stamp or passport, its
     photo smiling
back at him, presumably himself. He is always moving on, throwing off
restraints of name and place, his secret joy only to embrace the mute
presence of another tree or rock – a final reality he has always sought.

He did not find some magic art, cherished under fragile glass
in the world's museums, or exempt himself from time or chance.
We don't know him yet, nor his quest, because some things
can't be directly said, only hinted at. As one hand proffers up a ticket,
another pats a pocket for his wallet. Here he departs again,
changing but unchanged, with so much left unsaid, unless a poem
arise from his journey, unbidden from itself. He sees dark figures now,
their backs turned to rain, and many faces of the mind, sparkling lights
both cruel and kind; winging over cities of the world; so let these words
simply settle around him now, and create their mood, creating him.

The rain refreshes, even as it spoils an afternoon of wandering, perhaps
through autumn crowds. He has been to Istanbul, Cairo and Madrid,
then back to London. Beyond Lake Eyre, where he later touches down,

after doing what he always did, now seeks a twice deserted place.
One simply nods, says hello and lights through any town.

Like us, he also smiles with friends in front of local landmarks.
Like we must do, he conspires with clichés, rehearsing nods and winks,
fake feelings, *given* templates, those *de rigueur* merely most
received. Better to entertain the nimbus round himself,
patter of smooth then rushed syllables sounding from a carriage,
or hush of wings that lift above a runway. Let's say his suitcase
was always empty, and he just drifted on, without
name or number, always somewhere north or south
of *onwards*, his luggage the obscurity he shares with night,
and no forwarding address but *here*, always another *there*.

He feels something move him now, as he moves on: something oblique
yet tangible fills the world, as its true dimension: the quality
of experience itself; the 'poetic' inhering everywhere . . .
This thought breaks off . . . as he attends to a couple playing chess
at a casual café table. Notice how he creates an atmosphere
around them now, by merely looking on. A young woman's black
knight is captured by her lover, who sits behind white pieces.
The two are hunched, and still, as if time had stopped.
He deftly reads the board, their stratagems, but must say nothing.
Both think to checkmate, but dare not blink or signal their intent –
the paradox of love, its scoreless hurt; knows they also know this.

Spring might revive his steps. He has left new footprints on a globe
turning in its ancient gravity, home at journey's end; still a distant
hint of summer. He inhales being, as it inhabits him,
a common human wish as travellers say; he can't easily shed his origins,

so many coats left on so many hooks. Why is it, he thinks, that nature's
novelty is duplicated everywhere, while an inner hologram –
of memory and the greater world his senses glide – should appear
unique? All this survives as some internal map of being, a hand
      sketching
itself on to blank paper. But tonight he must depart again.
An aircraft roars beyond the fields, as he reaches for his luggage.
Soon best be gone and on his way: the train will hurry past
a new concourse of commerce and ambition, then tomorrow
conjure avenues that abruptly wake from sleep. He reads
each fresh page that turns him here, into a trance of presence,
eloping with the briefest passage of a moment, to elevate everything,
finally, back into a single life. Daylight is brief and never final;
while possible journeys one might make, or never take, colour in
      the globe.

It's best to respect untidiness, remaining true to compromise,
rejecting consistency as a bloodless abstract, a lesser good.
He considers this the best recourse and wraps his arms
around horizons. At their floating limits, the places he completes
by being there whisper in his mind: and he becomes that whisper,
now grounded in each moment's slippage. So he packs his case of air,
packs his face of smiles and frowns, and listens to his echoes falter
in some new hotel across the river. There, just like despair or joy,
everything is true, held in suspension, linking *then* to *now*
where opposites embrace. Back at the bus stop with the rest,
we still can't see his inward smile, though such details
fill the world. Intuitively, the crowd in any street knows more
than it knows, just as we do. And so the traveller with his case
steps from a tarmac, or stands in wonder there. He looks quizzically

at us, because the whole journey is imaginary, just another self
that sleep erased, hushed by the breezy din of morning. All his doubts
and doubles have already entered or alighted from their happy queues.
Tiny distant lights blink as night soars along a wing.

Another day unpacked, another month; autumn on the road again,
one of many; brief distances erased beside a lake; a new city.
Because his reflections are more resonant than facts, and more
accurate, only his next breath can make him real. He smiles
and spreads that smile across the sky, so the picture it creates
becomes his inward impulse. He knows that things exist
abruptly, without notice, and have no need of him to shine,
whether outwardly or inwardly. A jogger nods, a mother smiles
at children, walkers saunter past. Another paradox: they offer
purely random joys, predictably. A distant vapour trail wastes
across the toy blue. Although it spins without him, should wandering
dream his little globe up? Might he trace a final path of feeling,
clothe intangibles with knowing, as more clouds create vast distance
at the limits of the view, to rush past window seats on planes,
to float in glass, or glimpsed from roadways? As he flies off, always
returning to himself, an evening full of calm assembles, light pulsing
from below; more artefacts of miracle: their promise, being, erasure.

Birds in a Crowded Sky |

Freeway, Flyover and Back

i Looping out
set of keys again   path   front door   new breaking sun
no moon   suburbs fade in rear-view reverie
soon the whole journey clears   arterial threads pulse
to coffee   a living map of red and white cells   bright
duco-bullets sketch lights down a city's living map
cash and oil elaborate   minds on spinning wheels
each differently the same   smudge distance into speed
to freeze-frame at the lights   you blink to think internal
roundabouts and loops   this need to drive   itself is driven
multi-lanes of nervous systems   brainy feeder-circuits
an immense self-immersion in the one big fabric's buzz
of must-do things   urgent or undone   all living in
the moment   read history   where kids spray-can tags
on cement fly-pasts   a fast lane's white-line *nows*
are bullet blips   your space-capsule's escape velocity
arrows up past land-fill   twists of DNA coil past
vast flyover views   now do our tiny human egos count?

ii Looping up
you idle in top gear   raving thoughts do burnouts   drift at speed
with glassy eyes   where thump-mobiles wham
the air-gaps   utes gadget past   a tray truck looms and tucks
to tailgate on your loopy concentration   is any highway
utilitarian or some zany bureaucrat's literal concrete
auto-graph?   the journey is a signature of being here
never finally done   another little crash-site life
airbrushed from existence   duck to the safety lane
roundabouts again   and ramped up spillways
engines fanging down   trailing plumes of fast-tracked

time   whatever dumb luck gets you through
spaghetti junction   the take-away and service lane
slip past marching mono-culture plant protectors
a 4WD towing endless growth to rote McMansions
new dreams of suburbs streaming past

iii Looping back
the good life of anxiety   spirals round its own reflexive symmetry
a single continuous surface   your city's endless self   delirious virtual
Moebius twist   collective needs internalized   hands on wheels
but who knows who   or what   is driving anything   wrong way
go back   another day in the big day of forever   endless rushing on
of hours totalled with the daily bacon   home stretch in sight
any cosy suburb's love or loss   a domestic welcome
slip out of liquid speed   unbuckle seatbelt   switch ignition off
shrug yourself alive again   looming dark and moonrise
signal re-arrival and another day's survival   duplicated
down endless lines of doorsteps, drives and welcome mats

Slick

Waking Dream

Summer in Australia sleeps in oil,
as I pillow-punch to almost wake more
sand-raked headlights dream-cut to lights
beneath my eyelids, the scene widens like TV:
rich distillates from burning rigs spray liquid gold.

Flood to fields in hammering light,
bright engine candles, the desert prinked
with velvety explosions; as new lenses zoom,
a whole planet wobbles with soft rumbling.

Outside my room a motor sears its
studs blue, pushing stars out of the sky,
the waking sun our dreaming headlight.

From ancient shale beds, black lode
of buried ferns erupts again as oil.
Wealth pours down pipelines here,
mechanical parts flare madly as throaty motors
rumble smoke out. Drivers slam the doors,
time slipping down the glass, light emblazons
polished armour, hot enamel plates.

In tarry dark outside my window,
black seas beneath the night pour out;
under hard dawn stars, new cars rev up:
we race on, burning dreams and time away.

'Kelly at the Mines (1946)'

(Ned Kelly series, 27 paintings,
Sidney Nolan, 1946–47)

Arrested by a rope, you elope with sky
    and broken balances
        and hang forever falling:
your defiant tilt at flight
still armoured, heedless, headless.
Now jailbirds make your beard their nest.

Arrested by the sky, a starburst on the wind,
    after troopers, crows and horses tip
upended from the hue and cry of blue,
    you are always falling
    head over heel, you tumble down
    a delirium of hills, your scrubby ballet.

Arrested by the ground, all you know is how
you stumbled from the sky, an upside-down man
    at the bottom of the world.
Snagged in branches of the law,
    you bent their highest crown awry.

Arrested by the sun and earth, your colours deepen
    into mullock, stringybark and russet.
A dream exhumed from candle stubs
was dictated at *Jerilderie, a letter* to Joe Byrne.

Your helmet floats to rocky soil
where only night is safe, a final hiding.

Arrested by the cobalt,
far from the emerald cloudburst
where tears might have clovered into rain:
over pockmarked hills, smoke wisps,
        mullock-heaps beside a windlass,
your scribbled life is tracked forever here.

Arrested by all that binds or blinds,
        you bail the horizon up.
As piecrust fields bake in the heat of summer,
mica mines hint with fool's gold
        at your desertion from the sky.
Your shovel-bearded face remains un-graven,
        semaphores your nothingness in paint.
Un-hushed by irons you might wake a colony,
        your failure now a wilder ore,
        and defiance wriggles up from pigment.

Arrested by the floating shapes of rain,
        your mirage glides the surface of a lake,
        blinks from insect wings, quartz shards, smashed glass,
rivets on your mask are specks of golden hope.

Arrested by a chain and cuffs, with every stroke
        you flatten up against yourself,
the bars dissolved, mouth an angry slit,
        your bold knight's armour beaten
        down with flame and rage,
of black and crimson mettle.

The Rabbit-Proof Sonnet

1.
Fourteen clunky lines, an endless fence
With rabbit holes, ravage and excrement.
Our brains blighted by this bitter sun.
A withered foliage, chewed down to the root.
Wait! Is that one? Playing dead, by your shadow.
Don't move, while I get my gun – aim, and shoo . . . !
Grit and bulldust, endless empty skies: from shore
To shore, fence to fence, too many rabbits to evict,
Shoot or civilise. Free from mixo, hate, fear, poverty
And the lovely bleeding hearts of rabbit-hugging loonies
Bent on tut-tutting. *Traps, bait, snares, dogs, ferrets . . . !*
Fourteen fences now, miniature horizons,
Freed from gnawing pangs, and the *flies*!

2.
A rabbit can't help being a rabbit,
Nor I my knee-jerk need to lock him out
Patrolling in my 4WD, sweating like a shock jock:
China has its Wall, but we have risen
Higher, with eight thousand miles of twelve-gauge wire:
Impress a meaner impulse, protect The West.
They blew in on Australia Day, snuggled on a fleet
Of overloaded floating hulks, way back when the world
Was round. Still is. Touch of home, some sport and food.
Native species doomed, crops lost each year,
Victims to the long of ear, *Leporidae*, of family *Lagomorpha.*
Bright-eyed, warm and fluffy, victims in a larger trap,
Prick lost innocence, from some children's story book
Or nursery rhyme. In these stony times, evict them!

3.
Some drowned, all gaoled, some shot.
Soon they will be stealing my house, swimming pool
And rocking cots. So I've sealed
The ragged borders of this sonnet,
Where rabbits might wriggle through
The mesh or burrow under it.
No one invited that bunny here
With his lips sewn tight.
A vigil, waiting in a midday stupor
For more rabbit stew.
Or sitting in a daggy camper van,
Ping pot-shots at empty beer cans
Beyond the dust and mines:
Peering down the sites of these long lines!

4.
A whole continent . . . obscene with borders . . .
Our ugliest populists . . . bark orders . . . secrecy . . .
Pulling at our strings, politics of fear for . . .
Detention centres . . . in deserts of the mind . . .
Beatings . . . hype and drums . . . media blaa-bah! Both sides failing
      . . . punish!
Jumped the queue! . . . *ad nauseam*, the most abandoned and desperate
Dislocated, dispossessed, rejected . . . who arrive or barely do, half dead
On floating ruins of their lives. Blame the victims . . . of evil
People smugglers . . . suicide:
The earth's most raped and ravaged . . . deemed vermin . . . this idea
Planted in . . . the mind of the country of the kind, now this
      sonnet's abject,

Full of h o l e s . . . missing lines . . . more twisted razor wire . . .
Riots! and defence . . . Shut them out . . . with mental blocks
and paranoia . . . Build another fence!

The Wedgetails

Order Falconiformes, family Accipitridae, diurnal raptor;
for traditional Wurundjeri people, 'Bunjil' is the ancestral creator

Eagles!
In high summer's dreaming light,
        upswept on breezy thermals,
three circle whitewashed trees,
leaf-crowns seethe on northerlies,
        three dots melt above the green,
        as spring grass bends and new life darts,
their curved-wide wings enfold
        the earth's far sides,
on whisperings, on slip-rimmed stealth.

As smaller ground-hugging birds erupt –
warning shrieks from silver crowns!
Choughs and currawongs harass great shapes,
soaring to a higher clip above *muyan*, silver wattle.
Clouds float above
        the morning shimmer-gloss
where a liquid ribbon threads low hills.

Three melt over Yarra Valley dazzle-pools –
billabongs prinked with *biel*, the river red gum.
They climb to firestick lands,
on their feather-fingers glide
like *panketye*, the boomerang.

Eyes eight times keener than a swallow's,
        read fine prints from two miles high.
A life-long devoted pair
        escort their awkward juvenile

still eking out its meals, in tow.
Three fly across the prey's
        own cloud-reflecting eyes
as clear as tiny *djurts*, as petal-stars.

The larger female fully stretched,
        her head hinged low on turret neck,
        circles in a summer sky.
        Looking down,
her waxen cere is yellow-streaked,
        the black beak hooked,
razor-edged, for tearing prey apart.

Aquila audax, the bold bird!
From her slipstream-whittled torso's
        soft torpedo,
unseen, on fold-back wings,
                she plunges through
        her own swift shadow,
a lightning strike from cloudless blue,
        grass flattens as the sky falls.

Spring breeding displays are aerobatic:
the male stoops to check in flight
        when his mate flips on her back –
they elaborate high passes
        to link enamoured claws,
in plummeting corkscrew loops,
                free-fall.
Two eggs, pale white and yellow,

in their ragged clump of sticks,
    a leaf-lined, airy sky-throne.

Raptor means *plunderer.*
    The first hatchling
       tears the second chick apart,
until every bone is gone –
bolts its brother's beak and shell down.

    Back-turned toes are hooked
          as talons lift ripe softness up;
prey stiffens in an ice vice,
wedge-tail splayed to brake or balance.

All day without a single wing-beat,
    three are balanced on the light.
First silent shadows, shaped only by the air,
    they rise on warm sky rivers,
skim the apex of each season.

High above a wind-torn hill,
new crescent moon at sundown,
where *Bunjil* climbs his timeless dream-sky
and becomes *Kunewallin,* the Southern Cross,
at nightfall (called *Warepil*
by north-western tribes,
      with his consort
the bright star Rigel).

Bunjil's silver wingspan shapes the sky.

Soars
like a vast and stringless kite
across
the
rising
dark.

Domino and Tabby

Tin carport, bales of winter hay along one wall.
Underfoot at night, the cold cement is frostier than stars.
Before evening falls, I mix a bucket of lucerne hay for
our horses, days lengthening to spring. At night,
an owl swoops down in silence. Grave, folded wings.
Midnight hears a scratching at the walls, sudden
scampering of rats across veranda slats.
Almost spring, a spotty tomcat sleeks around;
then much fatter tabby, equally wild-eyed, mangy,
dissolute. I throw a bouncing broom
into a triggered pool of sensor light at 8pm.
What of 'Old Russell', our blue-tongue lizard,
who yearly brings the sun, and rustles
back to life from some safe crack?
In early spring, like first flowers, fluffy feathers
soon drift across the garden: blue wrens, lorikeets,
galahs, their too-soon-torn, puff-ball life.
Cats left by roadside, left to breed in dump-bin
bush. A pet for Christmas, past kitten stage,
no longer cute. They get bigger, meaner, feral,
revert to wiry, efficient killers. Try patting cats
like that, they'll tear your hands to bits. I set a trap
and 'Domino' slams hard against its sides.
Hissing, yellow-eyed with rage he settles on his haunches,
all his stretching wires taught, ferociously alert,
soft pads telescope with claws.
He has dots of white down his jet-black
facial mask. All things suffer, want to live, he says.
I put him on the ute's front seat; but what if he slips
out, all fangs and fury? Anxious, but we make it.

My vet, cool with the familiar *coup de grace*, tap-taps
his needle, and Domino is stiff; his worry-cage
now a little wire hearse. Back home, I dig a hole
and re-set for Tabby, before her kittens drop.

Hillside Views Estate

'The view' is innocent of meaning or money, good or bad.
No view yet exists, that anyone can see, but lovers see
mysteriously, just slightly out of view: warm feelings
line an agent's pockets, bright ideas go on Sunday drives.
'The view' is still a creek spilling its beans across
a muddy plain, just a trickle of numbers to a bank, where
cows as fresh as milkshakes graze on grassy notions
of the picturesque. A mortgage belt tightens on a hill,
but 'the view' is still aloof to arithmetic and claims
the whole spectrum where green takes off from blue,
splashing leaves all over its big eucalyptus palette.
You know, just looking semi-detaches you from nature's
rein, and roos key in a contract off the plan. 'The view'
can articulate its own views now, walk the cookie-cutter
walk of slabs and stakes, talk the string-line talk
of solid brick right round the *package*. It's all win-win
situations, plus backyard spa, raised pool and barbie.
What view would miss out, climbing the hillside
higher for a better look at itself? More blocks follow it,
but bricks stay put, plum-bob perfect. Walls extend
windows, sell more stories overnight, up the ante,
elbowing shy glimpses of a sexed-up sky right out
of the view onto daytime TV in a shuttered room.
White goods, ankle biters next. Hoppers bounce with
landfill, factory fresh. A puzzle pocks the pre-cast air,
mirrors dazzle perfect mirrors. The view is mature
and invisible: subtle replicas everywhere, so no-one sees it.
One rainy Saturday when the kids grow up, the view
just thumbs a ride due west, beyond the wired sky,
the freeway noise. The view moves on, not looking back.

Coathanger, The Opera

On Sydney Harbour

"Dear Everyone, *'Coathanger, The Opera'* is fast leaping
into being, now a month from opening night. As your Producer,
let me assure you, our backers and sponsors are clear:
no expense will be spared, to get things right. Advance ticket sales,
blanket advertising, a production designed to thrill, major talent all
signed up, dancers, actors, singers, full orchestra and chorus . . .
Technically, will be a dream; sets and costumes, sound and lights.
Think extravaganza, audio-visual delights and dazzling 3D animation.
Of course, I'm spruiking my shirt off tonight, that's my job.
So. Go for it! We have six weeks. Rehearsals start tomorrow!"

It's always like that; as a script consultant, I should know:
producers shake hands, keep things on track, stroke our backers,
stoke the cast. Always – on with the show; and so much more to do.
Hey – watch out, front of stage! Those giant, blow-up words:
'March 19, 2022', the 90th anniversary of the opening of the Sydney
Harbour Bridge! Hurry backstage, where musicians bash out
'World's Tallest Steel Arch', a new aria from our songster team:
"Steel arch, you steal the show. / Who'll cut the streamers /
for the builders and the dreamers / Bridge City, Bridge City, /
Leaping Port Jackson, Sydney Harbour, / Milsons to Millers Point, /
a thousand soaring seagull flights / from The North Shore to The Rocks. /
Yachts in flotilla tow their creamy lace / across our famous cobalt blue. /
Bold icon cloaked in stars . . ." and so on. I'm already humming, as
   the band
tries a flashy opening fanfare, then into the refrain: *"Steel arch, steel*
   arch . . ."
After rehearsals, I find my quiet little office behind the dressing rooms.
Did you know, that on hot days the Bridge expands a full
   hand-span higher?

I file this factoid away, for a line of dialogue in '*The Engineers' Chorus*',
There, pencilled in! Then stage designer Brad pokes his head around
my door: "Our new 'gelato-tinted' scrims are done . . . for the preview!
A lovely gauzy glow, all backlit! They look a total treat. If I don't say
so myself." Brad looks as pleased as Rembrandt, with a smear
    of pistachio
pigment on one ear. "Thumbs up mate!" and we make a date for lunch.

"Opening night: the show awakes! Footlights, curtain, and then . . . ? "
Rob and Faye are with me, as we sit down to our daily brain-storm
session with the script. "If anyone asks," says Rob, "it's almost
'nailed down', that's what we always say. But there's still plenty left
to muck about with." "Muck or fuck," sighs Faye, "Jeezus, what a gig!"
"Because the writing's never done, until it really is," I butt in quietly.
Rob, a veteran of many shows, suggests we might transpose an *Act* or so:
"You see," he says, "after the hoopla of *Scene One*, having hooked
the rows, then we can slow things down, provide background – flesh
    things out . . .
View *of* the bridge, then view *from* the bridge, on a huge
    descending scrim;
honking horns and noise, flash to six lanes of traffic, and the two that
    were once
tram tracks." Faye, our astute writer colleague agrees. She likes it.
"Let's throw in more pics of construction – at various stages –
on a background screen. Plus that famous Grace Cossington-Smith
    painting,
The Bridge in Curve, 1930." A good idea, we toss it around, and then I
    quote:
"*There! The proud arch Colossus like bestride* / . . . *and bound the
    strafing tide* . . ."

from '*Visit of Hope to Sydney Cove, near Botany Bay*', a prophetic poem
penned, in 1789, by Erasmus Darwin, grand-dad of the famous Charles.
"Yes," adds Faye, "we use that quote then steam ahead to 1815,
when convict architect Francis Greenway proposed to
        Governor Macquarie
that a Bridge be built to span the Harbour." Rob puts down his
        pen, poking
at his laptop. "Yup, found it," he says: "In 1825, Greenway wrote
that such a Bridge would, quote: 'give an idea of magnificence to reflect
credit and glory on the colony'." "Credit and glory, nice phrase," we
all agree. This will set things up for *Scene Three's* big dance routines.

"He derails the dialogue!" they shout, when we hand our latest script
revisions to the cast. They have to learn new lines, and director
Lisa frowns in sympathy, then soothes them. What a pro, I think,
as she pours new oil to calm them down, and carefully nods to me,
adding some changes of her own. As for the actors, let them bitch:
I fully understand, they do their best! I placate them too: "Hey, you
        look great
in those new costumes!" (It's full dress rehearsal.) Then whisk
        myself away,
stage right, back to my quiet desk. Could we have a running line
of script, displayed on a horizontal screen? Of commentary and
        history, to please
the buffs, while we get on with it – with more razzle-dazzle and
        show-stoppers?
I write: "In 1900 the NSW Government held worldwide
        competitions for
the construction of a bridge, but plans were abandoned with the
        close advent

of World War I . . . " that sort of thing. I ring our *Techies*, and get
the nod.
Our *Carpenters* can rig it up, and *Lighting* likes it too.

With more dialogue to come, I ricochet through a group of electricians,
then fly out to the foyer. Hey – nearly got whacked by some bozo with
a ladder!
Outside, in the street, I can still hear a piano tinkle in my mind.
I look up to the sky, imagine . . . there's a storm over the Harbour
and muted stage lights. Actors appear with umbrellas, one flicks
rain spots
off his coat and smiles, while a third stares moodily at our lead
vocalist, Janice,
who floats down on wires to sing '*Rain Over the Opera House*'.
Most in the cast have worked with Jan before, and having such a
seasoned star
makes everyone breathe easier. When she's on stage, you instantly
think '*encore*'.
Her lovely soprano lilts like cascading silk; and we have just
commissioned
a young 'wunderkind' composer for the score. Of course, at this stage,
it's all just jigsaw bits, no real sequence yet. Breathe deep, go back inside!

Scene Three is the really big one. Fay and Rob are on track with me,
thankfully, for such a dramatic moment in the script.
A brass band and full chorus on stage, as it all takes off
with our big stage number, '*Dr "Job" Bradfield's Dream*':
"*Dr Bradfield's on the Job! / Our most visionary engineer /
He dreams of new Sydney rail lines, / to further his career . . .*"
Bradfield, in formal suit and hard hat, steps briskly forward

to take the vocal lead: "*Yes, it's my grand scheme, in 1915, /
for our new Sydney rail link. / But why not build a Bridge? /
Let's also build a Bridge, / One of the best the world has ever seen . . . /
It's my latest scheme, / I'll make it real, an arch of shining steel . . .*"
Did they have hard hats back then? We best check! Anyway, in 1921,
Bradfield favours a single-arch design. Then, in 1922, the 'bridge
   bill' goes
through Parliament; with open tenders called. We work in dialogue,
for five new voices. First, *Kathleen Butler*: "Back then, I was an
   unsung heroine,
known as Bradfield's 'secretary' – but played a critical role, as his
   technical
co-visionary, and without me that Bridge might never have been built."
Then for Bradfield's three 'bridge boffin' helpers, of construction
and design fame: Lawrence Ennis, Edward Judge and Sir
   Ralph Freeman.
Terse feuds between Bradfield and Freeman, we feel, add
   dramatic interest.
Freeman: "You claimed that you conceived the Bridge alone.
Yet everyone knows, the true design was mine."
Bradfield: "But who had first vision, the steel to see to see it through?"
After this, Braddy goes to the very edge of stage, pleading directly to
   the audience.
Bradfield: "They named the highway after me! Construction began
   in 1923,
the first sod turned at Milsons Point. I earned my fame. I did
   not disappoint!"
Next, enter the *State Governor,* in high hat: "In 1924, the firm of
   Dorman Long won

the contract for our new Bridge. The price was exactly: 4.217721
   million pounds,
plus 11 shillings *and* 10 pence." *Chorus*: "Now don't forget the
   10 pence!"
The Gov.: "But cost blew out to six and a quarter million quid, not
   fully paid
'til 1988. Just like the Bridge itself, was Dorman's wait a – haha,
   Long one!"

Next morning, Rob, Faye and I, all slightly hung-over, still agree
that *'The Engineers' Chorus'* in *Scene Four* bristles with colour;
those proud granite towers; taut cables carrying workers to the shore;
'creeping cranes' edging ever closer, until, in August 1930, the two
halves of the arch touch for the very first time. The aria, *'Join Hands
across the Water'*, fully tweaked by our maestro conductor, is now ready:
*"Flags of New Nation, our proud land / unfurl from every hand. /
All crane our necks to see / how resplendent it will be."*
Twelve workers descend on slings, recall their toil, and their toll:
*"Pylons and towers, working all hours / Concrete and steelwork, /
We're doing the real work now, / perched high in the clouds, /
driving a million red-hot rivets in, / where 16 workers have died . . . "*
A rousing, celebratory refrain recalls the first train which steamed
across the Bridge, just before 19 more locomotives were all lined up,
placed end to end, to test the final structural load capacity:
*"Back in '32! Whooa Whooa, all aboard! / There's Dr. Bradfield
waving from a carriage, / as he steams past, join hands across the water,/
every son and daughter of Australia now swells with pride . . . /
Where our storage sheds once stood, / now stands Luna Park /
our new fun palace, lit-up after dark. / Oh what a Bridge! Whooa Whooa!"*

I've got the jitters again, so duck out for fresh air; walk briskly
down to Circular Quay, a worry-free world beyond all care.
See some kids are fishing here, who hardly even *see* the Bridge.
Grand spectacle is a risk! Those singers all dangling from masts;
our musicians in rowboats! We need more rehearsal time:
it was ever thus! And when the Director herds us back in,
for more close 'bonding sessions', is that a good sign, or a worry?
Still, our opening sets *do* look truly mega-bonza. Spotlights blaze
to centre stage; more dancers, rising from the floor; our big
show tunes brighten things up alright. Just go for it, we say!
Breathing deep . . . Now, I'm feeling calm again. Hurry, go back.

We've drafted our major central scene, including its
'Grand Opening Aria: Speeches, Ribbon, Sword', watching
it being walked through in rehearsals (while scribbling more notes):
"Jack Lang, Jack Lang, should auld acquaintance be forgot . . .
The swords were crossed, the ribbon lost in 1932, when Republican
ardour got the better of you. To correct your defiant stance,
Tory de Groot charged up in uniform, he dashed up on his horse,
before the official ceremony had quite begun! He slashed
that tape in two before you could, Premier Jack Lang!
So de Groot was then arrested, and the ribbon was re-tied,
and cut again by Lang, to mend his wounded pride, all to a
    21-gun salute.
'I did this thing for our slighted King,' said the incensed de Goot,
wearing his old Hussars outfit, and cavalry blade in hand!
Then de Groot was taken to an asylum, to inspect his brain;
convicted of offences, and fined five pounds. But de Groot,
had powerful friends – members of The New Guard, anti-progress
toffs resentful of Lang's politics – and the verdict was reversed.

That hard-line paramilitary clique, New Guard, almost went to war,
to stop democratic dreams they saw brewing in Lang's head.
By May that year, rumour said, the New Guard even itched
for a coup d'état, with plots to kidnap Lang and imprison him
at Berrima! Lastly, spare a thought for a fine old chestnut steed
named 'Mick' – roped into this stern history, with de Groot bestride.
'Mick', who galloped in so gallantly, was just there for the ride!"

It's only two more weeks to go, and we've collectively polished up
the *Grand Finale,* a sort of collage of linked mini-performances.
First, the big march-past, for '*Bridging Centuries*', then actors, singers
and band leaders performing '*World War II, We're on the Bridge*
with Anti-Aircraft Crews'; leading into more recent times,
with '*Dare-Devil Philippe Petit Walks upon a Single Wire*',
followed by some very special acts for the year 2000, the amazing
'Millennial Displays', then rousing '*Stolen Generations Walk*':
"Our 300,000 can't be wrong, we're crossing the divide,
to bring us all together, after all the tears we've cried,
you cannot whitewash history, now it's time to try
to heal the wounds and come together, to cross the mighty sea,
to face the truth and make amends at last can set us free . . ."
It all ends with a bang, of course – a blazing lightshow re-creation
of some favourite New Year's Eve fireworks displays:
    'Hanging Diamonds'; 'Waterfalls';'Blue Moon and Ring of Fire';
    'Sun and Endless Rainbow',
and as 2017 turns into eight, then nine, a final, cascading, fiery sight.
Everyone, hold on tight. What will be, will be . . . alright on the night!

And it is . . . ! Flowers rain into the floodlights as we all bow down.
An audience of saints and angels: the house rings with loud applause.

What a relief! More curtain calls later, then the Director thanks us
as we have another drink, or two . . . : "Allow me to hug you all
for tonight's wonderful opening! *Coathanger, The Opera* is going
to be a hit! Thank you, misters and sisters. Go and have another sip.
You've earned it. Just a little one, now. And we'll do it all again
tomorrow night! Blood, sweat – and cheers! Outside, we're all elated,
humming catchy tunes, blowing silly kisses, and shaking (shaky) hands.

Suburban Whistle-Stop

Before dawn light ticks us off for being late,
early birds have been awake for hours. Along the track
platforms are awash with shirts and frocks.
Off we fly, on coffee highs and half-chewed toast
as chirpy flocks, still ticket-less in flight, tilt down
to favourite roosting spots, and coo their day away.

An heroic sprint, and carriage doors click shut,
breathless as our train departs. Sardine-tight aisles,
find a seat and tap out texts; watch endless sprawl
slide into sight, past graffiti tags and backyard views.

There are 50 faces identical beside us. Spill out at last
to office desks, the building site, a dangled dollar.

Day's end, backtrack to dreamy green-belt bliss;
fuzzy minds dispel their daily doses of hypnosis.
Branches burst out song as we drift on sullen
auto-pilot to our rest. Now work is for the birds –
warm up downy doonas, silk a fluffy nest.

Audacious Finery

At the Writers' Day

For K. H.

At the writers' day, one writer said,
"I want to write an airport block-buster,
dripping with violence, intrigue and sex,
about a globe-trotting ex-hooker turned fashion model –
a best best-seller, to make me rich!"

Another writer wanted to write
"Issue-based books to get
young people reading again,
and help them think."

Another, with half a smile, wanted
to write "A very brief book, titled
'The Compendium of German Humour'."

A fourth declared, very seriously,
that she did not see the point of writing
anything at all, except for
"Important books, to change the world."

The poet at the writers' day
looked very seriously at everyone
for a long time, thought carefully,
and said, "I would like to write
a small poem about foxgloves."

Maxwell's Field

Before Scottish scientist-poet and invalid James Clerk
Maxwell (1831–1879) transformed our idea of physical
reality, there were material points in motion. After
Maxwell, there were continuous fields. Maxwell,
prophet of the digital age, is now everywhere.

Braw day, indeed!
Clouds gather over Dumfries and Galloway, as James Clerk
Maxwell, high on a hill, sees in one long glance the entire
broad sherrifdom of Kirkcudbrightshire. Walking, bathing
and skulling were tonics for a grave infection of the lungs,
and sharp joy for a devout man of science, seeing such
considerable works of mathematical nature and incalculable
deity spread before him. High above Castle Douglas,
an updraft brewed. Warm air rising from a lowland meadow,
rare winter sun. Maxwell sat down upon a rock, picked up
sharp shards nearby: a knuckle of brute quartz, and thought.

Turner's inspiration
A vast flaring, as through a mist, with light shooting gold through
water-sheets, and mist swirling up like Turner's vision. The colours were
one blue and daffodil braid. It was like a field, and light shone through
the screen of new impressions, danced in flecks and points of lightest
pigment: an optic dance of rain, of storm, of fire.

Maxwell advances
Maxwell trudges to my house, through winter chill (*braw wind!*)
as eucalyptus and tea-tree imagine themselves around him.
His outline sharpens, all at once. See the wasted face,
the long, pale invalid's gleam, dripping whiskers,
rough thistle sideburns, keen eyes raised to heaven.

First contact
Determined, he tramped new fields of kangaroos,
as *far* and *near* are entirely erased,
now *now* is digital, online, post neo,
simultaneously he's floating out from every screen.
He morphs through virtual space,
all his being's fictions gathered close about him
like a rain-cloak. In this dance of rain, Australia
now is everywhere, pelting down electrons.

Back to you, Max
Maxwell! Sparking face, alight in pixels,
the jolt along your wires, eyes charged with cosmic ping,
slips into slippage, between abstract waveforms,
see his face – say, *visage* for Scots gentleman – it warps
yet stays miraculously itself. Lopsided smile fizzes
straight down exchanges of new feeder circuits,
branches into branches, bends magnetic flux.
Our new century, to the Max. Downloading fast.

James Clerk, what's on your mind?
Maxwell! His face bounces over borders, transgresses
nations, from satellite dish to first, second, third and infinite
worlds. It's 'Well, well Max', he speaks of science, ultra-texts:
*"I ken discern no final certainty, yet the mystery is consistent
and can be made to serve us . . ."* – that's how it works!

Imagine now, time's arrows
"Hello, ye hear me? Hello, hello in the ether" – as Maxwell takes
the call, *"Aye, Maxwell here"*, and your logon spills him

to a billion consoles. Now Max is a well of deep pure charge
sharpening our screens, miraculously pulls up a zillion
zinging vectors into spin-out terms, each side of four
huge equal signs. Excelsior! Four Angels square the harmony
of chaos, dispose a screen of dots, into blips of info-load.
"Apply the constants! Learn from Ohm and Faraday!"
What a Gauss! His face is all equations now.
The key is *averaging,* to find a deeper structure there,
odd consistency of slippage, the very eye of chaos –
so the pattern holds, his face clicks into pixel dance,
into photo-real, sliding from the laser trays of our new age.
His sleek equations set the angels loose, to ladder up
and down the wires, the medium, the space: wireless.

That Scottish storm?
Reflecting how he would soon be caught comprehensively in
    an elemental
electrical spectacle, James Clerk smiles, miles now from Glenlair,
imagines how pressure lowers in the upper atmosphere.
Heat, he noted, was a 'delta' term: a sum of average
movement within particulate matter. Ahem! *(Phlegm, coughing.)*
Saw, in his mind, trillions cohere – rain droplets around seeds
of dust and ice, their crystals sparkle. *"All must coalesce
in swirl."* Yes, so it happened. Thick hail, close thunder heads!
He noted now a slight rotation of the clouds,
saw one band with scores of others in a line-squall, one big
air mass curl, all rotating. He smelt the first wind's buffeting –
air sucked in from highland cool. *"Nature abhors an, et cetera."*
Cold fuselage of pellets pings down. Felt the ice-shot sting
and rattle his bare neck. Blue *zeds* of crackling lightning

tongued sky with delayed booms! *"Ah, the charge! Mystery*
is the flash I will one day describe precisely. That is, equate!"

In high fever, Maxwell wrestles angels
Dancing skeins, white light,
took his hand to where matter was unloosed
and felt vast muscles test him,
instantly thrown down and back a yard,
torn from the air, the storm-head crackled open,
and tensed with all his mind at the arcing angel –
still held him down, many heads, charged fangs
rising out of inchoate matter he meant to tame,
streamers singed his hair as he wrestled with probing
leaders waving in the charge flux, little sparkling fingers,
envoys of the flash! *Round one, the angel!*

Domestic bliss, and games
The fever soon subsided, though not his lingering cold. Handkerchiefs
left everywhere, and dangling from his pockets. He took exercise,
forbidden now outdoors, but running in slippers along the upper
corridor, down the stairs into the kitchen, there to pause,
stir a pot of soup, then bound upstairs again. Catherine Mary,
nee Dewar, his wife, would sometimes laugh and throw a hair
brush at him as he passed the sitting room where she embroidered.
Technically, he was retired, the smallpox having weakened him
near fatally. *And coughs!* Yet, this was the most productive phase.
    He added
to his great works on Electricity and Magnetism. For an amusement,
set up a colour box, near eight foot long and painted black.

He invited neighbours to view the light dissected, so prettily,
into chromatic bands, in this odd coffin. *"Wee pet rainbows! Look!"*

Round two, Maxwell!
He steeled his arm in the hold, flipping up
and backward on his feet again – each note a separate
term he parsed like lightning – swirling chaos
of storms, lank hair whipping, almost floated on his back now,
his eyes upon the prize. *"In whilk there was such
fire!"* Angelic plurality of foci. The mathematic soul
revealed to him, was written bold across the sky.
And held it now, held its huge wings down,
looked directly into the very face of light. An answer
on both sides. A vast dance of equal signs, and *inside –
inside the flash* – pierced its very piercing with his mind.
With all his mind's mature strength. He held it fast!

Maxwell radiant
Fields spread out invisibly in three-dimensions
and propagate in empty space, without the need of 'carrier'
medium, the 'ether' theoretical. Fields have a strength
and direction at every point. Imagine any one of these
points; as single, stationary and negatively charged.
Each flowers into a sphere of outpointing forces –
becomes a radiant node – in turn produces force 'vectors'
at every other point, on the line of each radiating
arrow in this field. Electric forces between charges are
proportional to their strength, and vary as the square
of distances apart. The flash of revolution.

Maxwell, in high style
"Every Molecule of Creation is fathomless in its perfection,
And the wave-lengths are the same in each direction
Of the Cosmos . . ." (His poems, quite conventional
in form, but bold and ground-breaking in their scientific
subject matter, written daily at his bureau, strength allowing.)

Maxwell's gifts
Maxwell departs, as abruptly as he came to visit me.
Left at my desk four gifts, new fields cleared for each.
Left curtains billowing – no one escapes their era! –
and muddy boot-print on the stairs, for Evidence.
A great freshness throughout the house.
And all the doors still open, banging. Air!

Notebook, monograph J. C. M.:
This is not a static universe, all is transformed!
Motions of electric charge, they produce magnetic
fields; while moving magnets produce electric ones.
My equations unify and extend,
as continuous fields. A 'differential' calculus
must indicate the rate of change of functions
within multiple dimensions. This gives great
flexibility to mathematics. Gives shape to seeming chaos!
We can find the rate of change of fields *at any point*.
We can plot numbers for point-charge and how
directions change. We can plot the *curl* –
"Just grasp it!" – it's like tiny fingers curve
around a charge in space. All this, and more.

A seashell on my desk
His 19th Century's calling card, left on my desk.
It was just a small and perfect shell. He must have collected it
from long rambles along some elevated beach,
slipped in his pocket. It radiated spiral segments
from its compact bud of curves, with the mollusc's
carapace shaped like a tiny serving dish,
excreted in a life-slow gesture. This nacreous fan,
pink on the under-shell, with rainbows
clinging to the rippled ridges of interior firmament,
curved higher to a raised lip folded back,
where the animal's small life once clung to brine
and tide. Each arc of growth restated its logic of
uniform segments: 2, 3, 5, 8, 13, the 'golden mean'
of Leonardo of Pisa, called 'Fibonacci'.

Maxwell's second gift
An unremarkable foxglove leaf, slightly wet with rain.
Light olive of its chlorophyll, deep in the sub-tissue
which had raised up a velvet nap and pile of fine hairs, vegetate:
the whole array leans whitely, catching light –
tributary veins in common inclination
from the stem, to allow the rain to run, collect and drop
from leaf-tip. He must have torn it casually
from a flower bed as he came in from the storm.

A third gift
A small bar magnet invisibly changed the cutlery
arranged around a metal vase, also transformed.

And fourth . . .
In his own hand, some lines of maths: a *crystalline equation*,
beautiful, daunting – one of his original famous 20
later refined to four and fundamental . . . Sings silently, forever.

The Library in the Snow

The library in the snow sleeps under a drift of frozen
words deep in its white landscape
the library steps are hard beneath the roof-line
where first pale light drips from lattices

you have come here to browse
the text of storms, where shivers of a winter sun
melt back, mere shards of air
you have come to borrow something from this pock

of drops pattering down all that dissolves, is dissolving
as you enter, blue lightning seeps in the intricate sleep
of white trillions, turning sills to ice
chill filigrees of chance, weightless galaxies

float beyond your index here
still, no microscopic slice of infinity
duplicates in the library in the snow
where alphabets pile up crystalline pale fires

in leaping fractals where frozen spirals dance
so run your finger down these brittle spines
crazed with bright ice, insignia, crisp gems
consult coins of five to seven, then twelve sides spinning

into circles spun of lattice logic, from each point anew
new fabric bursts from frost-webbed fire
read each shield, crested with its numbers
where light makes lines of radiant craters

here phrases are arrayed in snowy glyphs
into pure petals of mathematics
and whole books float down to you
as silence softly falls outside and

cold drifts across a whirling world
read on, before you become absorbed
completely in yourself
read on before your fingerprints

fuse and splinter into one cold cosmos
then turn from these steps
turn from the library in the snow
see your whole self floating up

leave with your borrowed time
your spiral annulus, your six-sided helix
your pentagram, your radial web
your crystal key, your wheel, your star

Breakout from *Poem Central*

"Come on, through here!"
Then, suddenly, I see a window open
straight below my dangling feet,
where *you*, in dark glasses,
wait to grab my legs and pull me through.
"Thanks, Reader!"
We sprint to the laboratory,
where the poems are tested, genres dissected,
stressed, DNA-sampled . . .
given a Total Critical Workout.

"Quick! Get them! The New prototypes!" you say,
then steer me past a tray of glowing test tubes.
"It's time to crack the safe and get the codes!"
A last tumbler slips, finally *clickclickclick* . . . we're in.
But flashing lights, a siren shrieks!

Cool and unperturbed,
you walk calmly to the lift,
and press a big red button
that says *UP!*
And suddenly – we're on the roof
of *Poem Central.*

Security guards are swarming
                everywhere:
"Give up! Poetry's finished!" they shout.
"Every poem's been done,
there's nothing new!"

And release a flight of ferocious *dactyls*,
just as our rescue helicopter appears.

(As I imagine this, it simply happens:
the Prototypes, you see, have become *active*.
Their *terror-dactyls* can't keep up!)

Those tiny guards wave angry fists at us
below, as we zoom away –
into a brand-new poem
now waiting to be imagined
into being with *you* . . .

The view is breathtaking
from this big doorway to the sky –
more shining cities of the mind . . . !

When you turn the page,
thanks again, Reader!

Birdsong Far Away

(For 'The Buggatronics' electronic music ensemble)

I hear birdsong far away.

I hear notes like ice or hail,
a storm of coloured glass,
I hear elastic dragons playing blackjack in the sky
and rainbows sneezing synaesthesia.
I hear tin tacks on tram tracks ping
as small sonic fire-bulbs of glass
shower-shatter on a diamond hotplate.
I hear shots from a sonic catapult belt out
jade angels into hot tingling yellow triangles.
I hear jumpstart cat's eyes crack and implode
in pepper spots and black electric
puff-pots of doom-light.
I hear vast jazz clouds of ping and sizzle,
and jarring jasper tin-cans of clunk,
all weaving through a vast sawing spectrum of noise.
Was that a cloud of dissonant fuzz-bats
banging upside down
through a collapsed fire-drum of sulphurous octaves?

I hear spectral harmonics double-back to base,
with endless snake-bands of bass-treble-trouble
above radiant craters of syncopated fizz.
I hear tintinnabulations of onomatopoeic syllables clanging
the heads of mobile junk sculptures together,
then marching in gargantuan gong-armour jump-step
and clacking cymbal feet
bang bang bang over hard metal fields.

I hear the whining fibrous fibrillation of strings
and high soaring romantic filaments of fracture.
I hear shimmering chimes throwing frantic
base-lines of delay into fire-pots of tin lids.
I hear pitch-shifting jag-shriek through samples pulsing
out a déjà-vu voodoo drone cooking up new
sizzle-flits into steamy smoke-blats of light.
I hear filings of crunch-shatter flock
and blue dins of cracked feedback-dives unlooping
into sonic waves of saturation.
I hear fast-tracked sine-curving blips of speed-boat sunlight
pelting pitter-pattern dots of sweet brief sound-braille!
I hear pellets of patter, pockets of slap, toaster racks of snap
and attacks of drum thunder, all shudder out their lightning.
I hear a pock-marked splat sequences under lovely somnambulistic
liquorish blister-fits of shock-flak.
I hear sudden crash crescendos of ping-pong
flitter-float out of intervals of brain-waved brain-weave,
soaring in fortuitous formation of information overload
in overdrive. I hear sound-woven wooden
sunflower-sandals on the wing,
and polyphony proliferate in prolific pink fits
as earphones ring out phonic-frolics.
I hear the slow-dying dissolving decay
of sharps and minnow-minims
fluting into remnant ripples of flat-lining minuets.

I hear tiny tin sputniks in formation,
like micro moons orbiting a melodic invention do,

and treble toes tip-tapping to tap-drips
as electro-anvils drift out lost echoes into ear-shells.

And birdsong.
I hear birdsong far away.

'So Much Depends'

After reflecting on 'The Red Wheelbarrow'
by William Carlos Williams:

> *"so much depends*
> *upon*
>
> *a red wheel*
> *barrow*
>
> *glazed with rain*
> *water*
>
> *beside the white*
> *chickens."*

And not only 'upon', but 'in' . . . Carried *in* the wheelbarrow
to 'here' . . . (My wheelbarrow is also red, as it happens.)
Today, I use it to move a large, recently fallen tree
to my chopping block – after chain-sawing logs into neat,

manageable 'rondels'. (The barrow's wheel and trough,
or 'mechanical advantage', helps me overcome gravity,
which is ever with us, and makes my muscles stretch;
'rondels' my private word for small cut logs.)

Let's beg the question now: whether things can ever truly
be said to 'exist' as text, or within a poem? Or only
simply in themselves, forever beyond language?
My barrow, more accurately, is darker orange, rather than

bright red, a slightly shorter wavelength in the visible spectrum.
It is no longer *glazed*, though rain fell yesterday,
and things froze overnight, now thawed in early sunlight,
which does bounce from everything, before extending

85

indefinitely, far outside the poem, further into space.
No white chickens here, in my yard, or chickens of any shade
or mottle I can see. But cockatoos do swoop around, picking up
stray oats dropped by several horses, busy chomping

in this rural 'background'; their long faces deep in buckets.
The wheelbarrow, the rain glaze, and chickens
in that iconic poem seem perfectly materially present.
Williams says how real things are important, and implies

an ordinary beauty, simplicity, utility and value.
Yet all this is part of something much larger, extending indefinitely
to where you cannot know. Our expanding universe is already
stretching out both time and space, carrying that *wheelbarrow*

within its timeless photograph, its particular 'now'.
Poems make sounds in our minds – as one word
you read is erased by the next – within the cellular
network of our neural selves, that intricate journey,

we 'hear' our reading, a 'silent interior whisper of words'.
Things might also 'crystallize' into culture here,
in the way '*The Red Wheelbarrow*'
is iconic of the imagistic poem, now perfectly real.

Williams knew the Zen thing, of perceiver and perceived
as one, yet objects simply exist within his poem,
independently of any 'I'. The space between his short
lines is not just a blank stage set, but – as in classic

Chinese painting – an obdurate *object-like* emptiness, still
reverberating within the perfect clarity of his composition.
An axe leans to one side of the picture I create,
my chopping block set in a small clearing

between two silver birches replete with un-burst buds.
(It's *Spring and all*!) A soft under-slip of scattered
wood chips cushions my boots. In a green-blush
paddock, a post-and-rail fence punctuates this line,

slightly darker brown after yesterday's brief rain.
Certainly, the materiality of text itself exists,
as ink on paper, or pixels on a screen. I unload
my barrow, select a piece of wood, and *whack!*

sheathed with bark, it divides cleanly, and drops
beside the block, the new fresh wood exposed.
A shrieking white cockatoo lifts its yellow crest,
because nothing that exists is ever 'ordinary'.

Poems Short and Sweet

Overheard on bus
   "It was like . . .
   grasping at fogwebs."

Don't open!
   Locked suitcase on a beach.
   Inside, a tidal wave.

Your new SUV
   wheel-locked outside
the Commodification of Being
   Contemporary Uses of Criticism Forum.

Brief conversation with John Forbes
   Me: "After 1939, Earth's TV signals began
   streaming into space . . . "
   John: "You mean, Andromeda
is getting *Mr. Ed*!?"

Soviet Realism
   Boy meets tractor,
   girl as incubator,
   raise apartment blocks!

Dictatorship
   No bread on the table,
   giant portraits everywhere.

Oxymoron
    Military intelligence.

Shouted, in park
    "Woofgang! Come here puppy!
    Woofgang, Woofgang!!"

Alone Together

The Man Who Lost Himself

The man who lost himself woke up one morning,
and realised he had lost himself. Well, perhaps
not lost – 'misplaced' or 'overlooked'.
He checked all the usual places he *might be*,
throwing back the rumpled covers
of his bed, but there was only an outline,
a vague impression. Later that day,
he looked for himself under his chair,
then tried to find himself reflected
in the eyes of passing people in the street.
It's true, they all looked *like* himself,
but were clearly not. He tried to remember,
back-tracking over the week: writing a list,
retracing the movements of each day – to arrive
at the absolutely certain *last* place he was
before he lost himself. It was frustrating,
infuriating. He checked his wallet, took off
his shoes, and shook them, peering at the soles.
He read the name on his credit cards,
removed his jacket and looked
at the label for a long time. Perhaps he had
deliberately *hidden himself* somewhere,
as one hides something valuable, but had
concealed himself far too well?
Until, one day, while not even looking,
he found a note he had written to himself:
each word carefully underlined:
"Just in case you forget the place
where you hid yourself, you will find me
in the garden, behind the summer house.

In the sunshine, in the rain.
It's been a long time, but I'm
still waiting for you there."

Hanuman Society

Alpha and lieutenant chimps, doing troop deals
for dominance and status, our enduring model
for the disputatious lives of humans in a group.
Some apeman parent, pope or primate started it
in the savannahs millennia ago, trading influence
and politics in the grasslands, our making bets
on making it evolved. So, scratch your head,
who can stay impressed by the antics of our 'betters'?
Our social life a bit like making funky monkey faces
in the mirror, for the ultimate 'peer' group.
In the other tree house, beyond the intimates,
always the same old toxic crew, ideologues,
card sharps, and a dopey celebrity or two?
You scratch my back, I'll get your fleas, promote
to greybeard rank with red-bum mums to duplicate
the pretty and the prettier, and you can join my gang
if you look good, fight hard, or bring home seeds and locusts,
a top banana. Beware, my puffed-up coat, so silvery!
My war-like livery, doing noisy warning dance hops,
the nastiest go straight up to the top, cultivate best allies
in a larger dance for power, to our mutual cost.
So, walk upright, from your branch of our knuckle-dragging
family. Ambition? Drive a school bus, bake bread,
grow tomatoes. Do something useful, enjoy one day
at a time, sleep in the sun, hope for peace.
At least, do no harm. Eat your fill, bend an arm,
procreate, then drop dead. As usual, the Beta chimps
will dream up useful schemes, Deltas deputised
to clean up, while the Alphas grab the peanuts!

The Man Who Found Himself

The man who found himself was reading in the garden,
when a note slipped out of his book: *Good luck!*
Keep looking for yourself! So he handed out leaflets
in the street, posted photos everywhere. *If you see me, please ring!*
But they were of a younger self, so no one did. Certainly, he saw
parts of himself in *everyone*; but that was true of *anyone*.
The man who found himself tried crystal healing,
table rapping, ear-candling, sought 'faith' in every creed, read Jung,
prayed in a dozen empty churches, watched men in funny hats
and gowns swing censers, left shiny things at shrines.
After a bad dream, even inspected his local cemetery,
just to leave no stone unturned. His 'grand mystical quest', however,
took him even further from himself. Finally, he said, "I'm over it!"
And pinched himself awake! He came sharply back, woke up
from his trance. What is, just simply *is*, he saw: whether rock
or tree, a person. He *had been* all along. Still years left on the calendar,
when nothing's lost, there's no point searching any further.
He enjoyed the day, caught up with friends, did useful things,
exercise, travel, some gardening . . . The man who found himself
shook hands with himself, and got on with his life.

Flowers Nodding in a Vase

Cut to the root, the good earth having done
its best, the cool water makes them tremor
when we all sit down. A thoughtful guest,
who mourns her sole companion cat, cups
a flower in one hand, inhaling slightly bitter scent.
She breathes *how sweet*. Birdsong and
her brief autumn sing. Another guest arrives,
forlorn, his family having tired of him,
now lives alone. All hope now slightly out
of focus; the matched pair ache to end
with wine-coloured dreaming petals, dappling
smiles arranged above a flower-printed cloth.
We have herbal tea instead. They sigh alone, go home
separately. As flowers do, we also nod goodbye:
petals flurried in their vase still draw cold
water through thin stems. Their colours radiate
the winter light spilling over chairs askew.

The Tent at Evening

Dextrina amused herself by throwing darts, a childish task
hardly worthy of her skill. They thudded to the bull, predictably,
as she totted up her takings for the day, wondering
as she always did this time of evening, at life's trajectory:
now in Australia; so far from Georgia and from Europe.
Reflection was a luxury she allowed herself sometimes;
elation, often burnished, only sharpening regret. The sum
was satisfactory, as the public always found her act exciting;
among the best in Rosto's Circus. She put down her darts,
her money in safe keeping, with all that earned from Papa's
dubious ingenuity – to retire upon, perhaps, when her vision,
her reflexes and aim were no longer as fine-tuned or true.
Papa was a master counterfeiter who, when she was just
a child, had buried her sick mother then further engraved
his crooked life as they slipped from town to 'down'.
Though precariously, and always followed by the law,
they kept one step ahead. Eventually, in New Orleans,
Dad 'bequeathed' his little daughter to dear Uncle Rosto,
a kindly circus tout. Typical of Papa's fecklessness:
and of giving her a future, ensuring she stayed safe.

Rosto and his little troupe disappeared from Texas shortly
afterwards; off to Europe: touring Spain, then France and Italy;
always on the road, the itinerant life, pulling up or pegging tents.
Dextrina, as a new addition to his group, learned the 'carnie'
trade, first selling tickets for his fairground rides.
She pictured now her little booth, beside two bobbing zebras.
Country after country followed, and finally Australia.
She flicked another dart, just as Bruce entered. He was like
Bruce always was, on his way to dinner with the other acts:

face unconcerned, expressionless. He found her sulky, still
mooching round their tent. When she declined, Bruce just
shrugged, and left her to herself. Untroubled by her moods,
Bruce always seemed content. Indeed, she thought, the ideal
man for her. Dextrina stood before a mirror, adjusting
her reflections, hair and costumes. She had a truly lovely
figure: slim, yet tightly curved. Sequins clung to breasts and hips;
her eyes dark twins of fire. At first, old Rosto had suggested
the trapeze. Apex of a human pyramid? An acrobat perhaps,
or even the high wire? What might best suit his niece . . . already
such a lovely athlete? Before they could decide, awe-struck
Pedro made his bid, after seeing her tumble with the warm-up clowns.
Hand on heart, the suave knife-thrower Pedro wore Dextrina down.

A favourite song now welled about her tent; then saddened her.
"My world, his world, our world, is mine and his alone . . ." sobbed
a soulful singer. Ah, Pedro! She relived her own long journey:
first her mentor, then tormentor, with his fine-boned
Latin face. He taught her all his skills, but soon the student overtook
her former master. They exchanged roles: with Dextrina now
flinging the blades, and Pedro strapped to her revolving target.
But such a showman! Always grinning in defiance, at all
life tossed at him. And how they made the crowds roar!
Ally-op! sent both man and wheel spinning. Then *Whoosh!*
daggers flew to wild applause! He trusted her, of course.
Her accuracy; when she raised her hand, every missile
true with love. They were artists first, and in accord,
beyond mere rivalry. As Dextrina lit his candle, it flickered
for a moment; cupped in tender hands. She almost wept,
to recall how Pedro finally met his end – in the choking,

vice-like grip of 'Titan', the brutal circus strongman.
For Pedro owned one fatal flaw: always a ladies man,
he could not resist a pretty face, or casual dalliance.
Rolling in the hay might be a game, but one night
behind the Grand Marquee, blasé Pedro threw his life away,
indiscreetly dallying with the oaf's flirtatious wife.
Dextrina smiled. She *understood* how women could not
help themselves with him. Such a charmer! Well, perhaps,
some jealousy: remembering a certain throw she deftly skewed,
which peeled a sliver from his chin; another toss had clipped
his ear. Pedro was the first, but not the last; each more
ardent than the one before, who doubled as assistants.
A little shrine inside her tent was mounted with their photos.
There they burned again: all her much-missed husbands.

A kookaburra laughed from edges of a country racetrack
Rosto's Roving Circus had lately pegged with tents
and parked with vans. The crowds were steady here,
a stream of farmers and small-towners, all starved for fun.
Dextrina picked up crumbs of local slang from punters,
to spice her act. "Don't just stand there like stunned mullets,
give Bruce the clap, you drongos!" Then whispered down
to him: "Don't move even a fly's fart when I send you spinning."
Of her tragic troupe, her eyes and heart fell most on Raoul,
her sixth and truly incandescent, who finally broke her heart.
She looked into his searching eyes, unsettling from his
portrait. A fire-eater in his prime, and prone to drunken rages,
Raoul was almost forced to leave the show. But Dextrina
pleaded with her uncle, "Please, just give him one last chance.
One final spin at keeping clean!" Raoul became her tender

number six; one whose faults and wounds proved too deep to mend.
If Pedro's fault was chasing skirts, then Raoul chased pure fantasy.
He made up infidelities; and imagined Dextrina hid affairs.
Finally, in a fit of lurching madness, Raoul climbed a shaky
ladder to the Big Top's wire cage; swallowed petrol, struck
a match and leapt – Raoul's final act, a drunken ball of flames.

Left devastated, numb for months, her former strength
a blunted edge, Dextrina volunteered for 'the cage of death'
in croc-filled Darwin rivers, not caring if she lived or died.
Why have I fallen for so many reckless, crazy men! Her tears
streamed again, and she wiped them on her sleeve.
She wanted no more pain: had learned her belated lesson!
More silver sequins moistly gleamed. But everything
had changed with Bruce: by contrast, so steady and prosaic,
the very opposite of wild. How might Australians say it?
Dextrina had a stab at using local slang; all those funny sayings
picked up touring 'in the sticks'. Bruce, *with the personality
of a roof rack*. Ha! *As much fun as a rubber boot full of treacle.*
Yes. *With the mental agility of a bathplug.* She laughed aloud,
and felt much better. Still, Bruce had his uses. Good at pegging
tents; he could even cook! And handsome, brave, so calm:
nothing ever bothered him. Feeling lighter, Dextrina played
their cheerful music: she sang along, to the glorious clowning
baritone: "*Figaro qua, Figaro la, Figaro su, Figaro giu . . .*"

To improve their act, Bruce grew a beard. No need for a barber's
shop! Thrilled by his seeming unconcern, the patrons laughed
then cheered. Close shaves, indeed! Turning faster on his bull's-eye,
with each near miss, more whiskers dropped. He might well have

been sunbathing on some beach! That first day she unstrapped
him from the wheel, Bruce had whispered, "It's a living."
Now grief had gone, it left her changed: with a sort of sad,
serene detachment. She looked down at them, hoping she would
never strike a seventh flame; opened up a velvet case, took steel
into her expert hands. In turn, she gauged the heft, the balance,
flipped them overhead; she spun about, catching each mid-air.
Practice for the night concluded; she wished all hurt adieu.
In turn; she blew their candles out. Yes. *Bruce, for now, will do.*

Poems Short and Sour

Overheard, two young men
　"She gave me
an invisible jolt."

Global warning
　Icecaps melting.
Snow on the pyramids.

The view from Blind Freddy Peak
　Why is the world
always ruled by *creeps*?!

Alcoholic, RIP
　Once the life of the party,
now liver of the departed.

Architects at the pool
　Last one in
has a rotten schemata!

Surreal awakening
　Childe Roland to a cold shower came.

Earth 2050
Frozen Sahara, the Arctic boils.
　Above underground bunkers,
last Mars-base signal fadeout.

Freudian slipper
　"Hand me er, my er, pipe, dear."

Bent piano
    A mist of white noise. Torn shoes.
Bug grit. More blue days.

Homages, Hellos and Headshakes

Poem for Dylan Thomas

"After the first death, there is no other"

Three thousand miles from Swansea, you raged
and gentled scores of spotty kids into poetry.
Better I had studied micro-biology, re-engineered
a slum or built a fortune. Better deaf to your
whisky-neat, organ-toned vocals
and unmade bed of a head hammering
through records, books and daisies.

You pulsed a sappy, libidinous Welsh-choir
hymnal of soaring loss and wonder,
taking all the registers by surprise,
including sales, in a brief counter spend-up
against poetry's usual genteel poverty.
You even got away with surrealism,
amidst the reedy-rush, spark-eyed tidings
of seabirds waking from lovely small-town
rhythms made more rhapsodic than real.

Yours was a lyrical hypnotism of voice:
Welsh cadences echoed everywhere about
my boyhood room. Straining at the starlit bud,
swept up in your gloriously orotund solemnity,
your magisterial, oceanic-surging and rhapsodic
rhythms it was poetic suicide to copy . . . That nice teacher
who got me started, when I was just 14. For some
jejune scribble, rewarded with a book and hooked for life –
taken on your long-legged bait, my bad-boy balladeer!

Better to have put that artfully pickled sprite of poetry
back into its dissolute bottle, before your *DTs*

really shook me up! Then long drift of shipwreck –
whether into pubs or publication – a 'career'
eked from handouts, workshops and chapbooks.

But I confess, I never wanted to be anything but a writer.
You pugnacious bard, you much-loved bawdy
beauty, warned how time is forever flying – moonstruck
and gone. Whether high or dry, love is seldom kind.

After the first review, there is always . . . another!

Charles Dodgson in Cheshire

"The Dodgfather of modern literature" – James Joyce
(Dodgson used the pen-name of 'Lewis Carroll')

He heard her mewing, quite unmistakeably, outside the highest
window of his college library. *There!* stranded on a shaking
branch, in a large oak tree. Charles Dodgson put a much-thumbed
book on mathematical lore aside, intent on helping the poor cat.
'Minette' leapt into his arms, quite rescued. In his rooms
that evening, she was offered milk and fire's warmth, watched over
by her new fond master. Dodgson was a doting friend, and enjoyed
this 'social climber's' company for almost two full years;
fed with cream, indulged with toys, allowed to scratch the legs of chairs.
No wonder Charles was quite perplexed when she disappeared – for that
is what she did. One day, there she clearly *was*, upon her fluffy mat,
the next day *wasn't!* 'Minette' proved a roamer, a true gypsy. Dodgson
searched, and as more days turned to night she failed to return.
    He became
quite fixed upon this all-consuming quest: only to find her! The
    full account,
not widely told but full of marvels, begins in such a simple way.

The obvious place was in his rooms; to open every cupboard,
look into stairwells, down coal chutes. Next, 'The House',
serried pews of Oxford Cathedral, grand quadrangles of Peckwater
and Tom Quad. Along with his hope, Charles pinned up
posters round the greater shire, from Jericho to Cumnor Hill,
complete with his own pencil drawings of the tubby truant.
Perhaps someone had spied her, underneath the city's
dreaming spires. Charles sketched her breed and style thus:
"A British shorthair tabby, thick of coat and broad of cheek,
her lips curled upwards. Sometimes called a 'cheese-cat', because
first bred in Cheshire dairy country, where cheese was moulded

like a cat in olden times. Have you seen her?"
Charles rowed the 'Isis' bends; calling for Minette.
He trawled Oxford Canal, then waterways of Iffley Locks.
At Folly Bridge he showed his scholar's frown, and spoke to
a local bargeman. "A downpour yesterday may have swept
your cat away, sir." Though Charles had all the spilling rivers
dragged with nets, his Minette seemed spared. Only
sundials and gold fob-watches were found among the reeds.

Perhaps his leg was pulled, in reference to credulity:
on the first day of his quest, when some Oxford wag
assured him truly 'cheese-cats' of the Cheshire
ilk were want to roam, predictably, back to their origins
ever smiling, where fresh cream was plentiful. Dodgson
took a train to Chester, on the river Dee,
quite close to his own birthplace, the parish of Daresbury.
The first morning of his stay, he heard this rumour:
a huge and shining cat was often seen in wilds of Delamere Forest,
near boggy Hatchmere, and so brightly glowing it could
be seen for miles round. He camped by the largest lake there,
his steady spyglass trained at heaven. But, to his chagrin,
like fumes of Delphi arising from some deep seam of rock,
only updrafts from a local 'kettle hole' leapt above the trees:
into incandescent feline shapes, which quickly disappeared.

Cheshire boasts the loftiest of landmarks, Beeston Castle,
built long ago by crusading knights on their return to English soil.
While resting on those compact battlements, Dodgson read of how
enchanted felines, long of legend, were destined to live according
to their names. 'Minette' meant coquettish girl in French:

a flirt, or free spirit if you must; a tease, most playful to the last.
Should he, instead, have called her 'Faith' or 'Constance'?
Would she have purred far closer to his side? In the third day
of his tour, Charles met a Cheshire scholar, biographer
of the famed John Milton, and they discussed the fatality
of names; then truancy of certain short-haired English cats.
"You know," the scholar said, "sublime Milton, just like yourself,
possessed a cat that caused him much distress, after it too
went roaming. The feline's name was Paradise, I think."

"*That dashed cat! I admit, it vexes me, I would greatly like
to see Minette securely ribboned, belled and saucered!*"
Such were his inward thoughts that night, as Charles took up
a deck of cards, prescribing Patience for his mood –
just as a playful breeze found his window open,
winnowed round the room, and sent the whole pack flying.
The Queen of Hearts danced past his eye, suspended briefly
in mid-air. He sensed Minette might be close to him
tonight; almost close enough to touch. This was truest insight,
one most profound, for he searched for something he had
never lost! Minette, indeed, had become his pure 'Idea'.
Still invisible to him, she presently sat upon his head; smiled
inwardly; her ears flicked at every clink of glass, as travellers talked
downstairs. She tiptoed nimbly to his shoulder, seemed
purring to herself, settled quite unseen by Charles
upon a mat beside his feet. Minette was always happiest –
as Pure Idea, or Speculative Entity – to transform into
a rising mist, a poem, an aspidistra growing in a pot,
a question mark upon a mellow page as Charles read,
the pillow on his bed, or rabbit leaping down a burrow . . .

Little wonder, then, *That dashed cat!* remained elusive.
Patience placated, Charles went downstairs, where he
met two jolly cider-sellers; both tipsy, telling clever tales.
Charles joined them by the parlour fire, overcoming his reserve.
"Gentlemen, perhaps . . . " he paused, "perhaps you have seen
a cat about your journeys?" One playful merchant winked
and said: "I spied a short-haired tabby curled up on a chair –
a giant cat with whiskers long as the Kaiser's moustaches;
but I admits it was a day I'd drunk three jugs of cidey!"
The men laughed. "Ha now Bert," said the other worthy,
"Now, come to think of it, I did sees one meself, sleeping in
a rowboat yesterday." Charles sighed, resigned to certainty
he'd met two amusing liars, who might entertain, but hardly
help him. Then, to pass the time as pleasantly as time allowed,
challenged them to name three things, any things at all,
which he might weave for them tonight into a little tale.
His listeners agreed, and surveyed the room for inspiration.
Charles waited in his chair, while Minettte – though still unseen
and coiled warmly by his ear – caught all his passing thoughts.
"Alright!" said one, "The two things I choose are . . . " he paused,
" . . . a cuckoo clock, like that one upon the wall, and a parson
named Lutwidge." His companion added: "And the third, a band
of India rubber, of the sort most useful for bundling letters up."

Firstly, in his tale, Charles introduced a cleric, a clever man
named Lutwidge, worthy in most respects, but flawed with this
    one vice –
an overweening and meticulous regard for punctuality and keeping
proper time. "If this good cleric's watch was but a second out,"
Charles told the cider men, "he'd erupt with spleen, and dash it

to the floor – a good timepiece reduced to bouncing springs and cogs –
only later rueing his literal waste of precious time!
Lutwidge," Charles said, "listened to each chime and tock, removed
the backs of gold fob-watches, to scrutinise their movements.
But no timepiece had ever satisfied his quest for rare perfection,
albeit of a temporal kind. Until, one day he glanced up at the wall,
where his cuckoo clock had kept the hours for decades.
The clock was always true, its ticking and display quite faultless,
and so had *stayed* unnoticed! So Lutwidge fixed that clock – pendant,
bird and all – onto his very person; secured to one wrist, with a strip
of braided India rubber. People smiled and shook their heads,
starting when the bird sprang out upon its spring.
But the little cuckoo bird, whose name was Flighty,
after searching everywhere, knew she had misplaced,
somewhere in her cogs, a *single lost second*. She also knew
the fierce moods of Lutwidge who, if she proved wrong,
might toss her – pendants, spring and all – 'into the middle
of next week!' So the little cuckoo bird took flight. Her tiny
wings became a blur of light, in freedom of the open sky.
For, in short, good gentlemen, my moral is: *Time flies!*"

It began with something quite impossible. Soon asleep
that night, Charles dreamt he stood beside a giant billiard table,
with velvet nap of undulating meadows. There, he joined
a walking party, and set out for a lake, where a packet yacht
departs its sparkling centre. As billiard balls, from time to time,
splashed harmlessly into the peaceful water, Charles found
himself seated on the upper deck, to watch a magic lantern show;
the velvet curtains slowly drawn aside. (Of course, Charles still
lies snoring in his bed, unaware he is both peaceful tale and author.)

A spark of golden light pulsed upon the slide, everything
engulfed in darkness, as his boat with wings rose past endless
moons and stars. The light was brightest near the constellation Felis.
Though still asleep, Charles somehow recalled these lines:
"When nature, our grand mother, with the aim of eternity in mind
Thought wearily of being alone, she contrived a perfect masterpiece
To keep her company, with spirit, beauty, force sublime . . ."
More lights dance in points of fire, where a figure basks
in radiance, naked on her red *chaise lounge*, at the very apex
of the stars. The Most Illustrious Madam Everything! Irresistibly,
she beckons us, as Charles sees a smiling cat, now just
a smudge of time, recline beside Her Pulchritude. "Ah," (still
in his trance) "is that truly my Minette, for whom I seek,
or just another starry stray?" He bows low to Madam Everything,
who flies into the air, suspended for a second, but . . . Charles woke
and rubbed his eyes. *That dashed cat!* he half whispered;
as velvet curtains closed at last on deep and dreamless sleep.

Come mid-morning, Charles staggered from his bed,
to be briskly met downstairs by the lost Minette. She looks
at him and mews, as if she'd never been away. Her whiskers
coated with fresh cream, supplied by a kindly kitchen maid.
Minette, at last! He clasped the purring vagrant to his breast.
Such joy! Just on a whim, she had restored herself to him, from
      some rare
and philosophic realm. Meanwhile, the inn grew rowdier, patrons
called for tea and breakfast plates. A lively group of Montgolfier
balloonists had just floated down. Charles was amazed to see,
tethered in the misty dawn outside, balloons of every shape and size:
swaying on the slightest breeze, suspended with their baskets

and gondolas. Charles in buoyant mood, having found Minette, asked
to fly with them fast back to Oxford. So, untethered and aloft, all
taking leave of earth, a morning breeze elevated more brightly
coloured dots, slowly circled by a tiny talking bird called Flighty,
higher to her chair of stars, where Madame Everything reclines.
So ends the tale of friends lost and re-won, with no more tears
or sighs, or from the wayward air the slightest whisper;
nor parting smile, just clear sky, without a single whisker.

Elvis Fountain, Graceland

Tourists lean against the lurch of stopping buses,
tumble into Graceland's ruin. His statue seems to croon:
Thankyouvurrymuch, into stars and doubling blues,
jolts a single dark-lashed look, the full force
of charisma's ache. Young Elvis still mines sex
above a mansion's manicured lawns.

Fountains plash and amplify his fame's eternal flame,
spilling milk and rose. We skim lucky coins for him
across the tranquil liquid sky, as fanlights frame
his sideburned head, crying down
to base adoration: two kiss-polished stones.

His fame trails an endless silver wake, as ducks with shining
bibs bob up. Brassy water-flutes deepen his patina
with angelic mould, dusty purple seals his reign.
A pout becomes a cloud in the pitted patter of lost sobs:
astrut the fractured mirror pool, he is said to weep real tears.

Oh, if he shook his head it might rock down from sculpted
light and roll to new splash hits. But he will never topple
or un-engrave himself. Devotees arrive to take the full
house tour. Graceland weaves and splits across his multiple
reflections, exporting tribute-shows around the globe.
The awestruck king goes gold, goes platinum, goes stone.

Michael as a Glider Plane

For poet, writer and friend to many, Michael Dugan (1947–2006).
Michael was lead vocalist in the 1970s King Hippo Poetry Band
and enjoyed "the weightless silent uplift of gliders". This tribute poem
was read at his memorial at Melbourne's La Mama Theatre in 2006.

On the runway: Michael, with his arms outstretched.
He's a glider now, towed by a golden thread.
Time slips under him, he's taxi-ing, gaining
speed, his outstretched arms are wings –
his walrus moustache streams like the wind.
King Hippo – king! gliding way above us,
Michael is a glider, lifting higher over treetops
and these toy buildings, up through clouds,
as all the roofs of Carlton rattle down,
like little coloured dice shaken from a cup.

Up there, above us, gliding –
above La Mama, in big unwinding circles,
        Michael turns a few slow arcs
then soars above the streets he knew so well –
he says goodbye – salutes, clips off . . .

Balanced on the knife wind now, the Earth
        a remote, black fatal teardrop,
        just diamond dust on velvet . . .
lifted up on music, on fractured, feeding-back guitars,
drums beating out of time, rhapsodic wailing song –
                with starlight on his wings,
Michael shakes off that plaything, gravity,
        and soars and glides . . . now far, far out

Michael tips back his head and laughs,
    gulping down the stars,
his walrus moustache still streaming on,
now joined by other poets, wingtip to wingtip,
soaring on, together glide
        the whole vast, dark cooling night,
    with Charles Buckmaster, Ken Taylor,
    Alison Hill, Geoff Eggleston,
    Mal Morgan, Shelton Lea . . .
into that spark-spitting Catherine wheel:
spinning gunchamber roulette
    with a million suns,
daring it, to where the stars are born,
    into the very eye of chaos,
    King Hippo, king!
Michael tips back his head and laughs,
a full unbroken laugh, and laughs and laughs.

Hell's Bells!

Scene: Sydney Journalists' Club, Ultimo (closed 1997).
Its Gaming Room and Kenneth Slessor Memorial Library.
Slessor's Ghost: "In this vanished building above the library named after me,
between whirring tokens in that miserly fruit machine
below your bending elbow . . . Here, many punters died small deaths,
clenched teeth and sucked in smoke as crisp as headlines."

1. Five Bells
Return with me again, a fellow wraith,
and float up through the floor
where cigarette smoke cold-shoulders the light
and creeps to dingy stools. Little pay-outs coldly
splash the machine's cash-tray. No furious gambler at the bar,
drowning in a schooner of beer, likes to hear the pokie
they had primed all day finally slide its silver lode
into another's pockets, accompanied by astonished laughter!
More than once, left stony broke, has some investor
lifted his offending 'bandit', while still whirring,
and thrown it through an open window, down into the street!

Did they ever think of me, below them clasped in vellum,
here where profitless chance presides, anchored in *louche* change?
I have not gone from the earth,
but am that wraith beside your hand always,
that trips the handle, or at button's press
launches fortune towards treacherous lights.
Scribes that purse their lips to mute zeros spoke
my name, enunciated ports of space above
a notebook where shorthand thunder's heard. Are you
shouting, editor? Contorting your face into smiles

for scratch tokens that have flowed from some quill's
petty dance? Shout louder, buy us all a drink!

2. Five Plums
I hear the same clichés, and bells or lemons
whirr, jacks and aces click, cold splash of cash
lights up just in time. But no player here can ply the truly
awesome reef, though your dumb machine of flesh
is primed. I float about these faces and despair – our finest touts
record leviathan deeds in pygmy print! In bygone days they
stalked the lazy five and gambolled: 'Harry the Horse'
and 'The Squid' were always good for a loose quid, inking
their outlines into a history of winter rain and tokens, whirling
out like time does under foam – amber slops where sunset
and regret foment some last daring spree, an entire paycheck
in an hour! The flower of our fourth estate, with buttons
all awry, after reeling from the Loo, and pockets inside-out.
Oh perfidy of this debased age, hear mere ruin clank behind
low-ceilinged temples of the press! *Five tumblers whirr!*

In Sydney, by the lugubrious gasometer,
I thought about your final days, Harry, and of my own.
You, a secret poet, press-ganged into dross,
until the end a three-bottle man, and each more bitter than the last,
you slipped on a piece of soap while climbing from your bath.
Sub-letting talent for a safe life in the suburbs couldn't save you,
and, alas! what delirious sonnets from Cairo or Tibet? But they
were living, and I vowed to write them for you, those frames
and shapes of words that had perplexed our youth. At first, what
sea-lanes and weather fair! Seas like inspiration, spinnakers aflame

beyond the kicking bow, air cruel as thought! What nitrogen
wicking down from lightning nurtured your see-saw bed!
It did not matter, the loneliness of our voyage, the light
house keepers, and shore men tending calm out of the deluge.
All of daring was the tide we risked to put our history right.
Oh horizons dark and bucking under foam, called forth great souls
out there beyond the reef – legend's storm-lashed throng –
who ignored cloudy warnings beyond harbor or dry-dock,
far from petty trawlers steering schooners onto coasters.

3. Five Grapes
How have I sunk? A ghost now smoking from a plaque, this genius
of brazen machinery, that suggest always one last chance till
you're truly shipwrecked. Take this glass! Aye, lost, and all at sea!
After each new voyage I returned with hands full of wonders,
ferried pearl to the first swine at the dock. I was rocked by eternity,
that fearful sob, yet the slap and sting only stirred resentment, and *Time's*
own critic was a reputation-robber, unable to abide subtle diction
in outposts of the Bloke and Cobber. Your bouquets are cast
on silence, an apparition on the tide, colour and petals drowning here.
These landsmen look to merchant ships, and think much more
of slick and artless captions on page four. It begins to pall, Clink!
It begins to pall, Clunk! So you drink, or wear expensive clothes,
cultivate a delicate taste for china, a napkin's edge, until you hate
yourself, even throw your wife's best silver out the door,
a total unmitigated boor. And such it was: drowned by harbour lights
and ragged squalls beating on these sullen panes of fancy's toast,
spillage of a season, how I gasped at meaning, could not feel the air
inside my chest, yet grasped at straws, and bobbled out a ghost,
a cork on dandy tides. Whose loss is this you play again?

Will you bet your birthright for some bauble, mere sullied thing?
If I could sing who now am gone, could my purpose give new breath
to you who ply the ebb and flow, yet stay alive to wonderment? Could
   I seize
all loss? Must you become a ghost to answer, and to *answers*?

I look from Captain Dobbin's window in this run-down joint,
at points of darting neon, the diamond and the hearts aflutter,
the spin of lucky lights and not-so-lucky, now plucked
from Hell like some Flying Dutchman who sinned against his gift,
banished to the spindrift and the spume, this beery room,
while my heart is all at sea, a passionate roar of breakers –
far from bells, five lemons, handfuls of jacks. Five again!
Petty cash cannot pay for this, five bells coldly paying out. *Five Bells.*

4. Five Peaches
But I saw again the desk, the spike,
the sub-editor's in-tray gorged with flotsam,
and you, Harry, but a copy person, a cadet again,
that night we covered Morebank, so green
that sap ran from your pen. Your body ridiculous
in a trench-coat, a notepad in the lining of your hat,
aspiration confined by the lasso of its brim.
We covered the mid-week dogs, a trenchant
barking out of air and down the line and lug
of some poor mug at the office, then straight off
to the press! You delivered halting lines but made
the grade. Then how we talked, nor balked to whisper
secret things, our sonnets illumined the creaking stadium
by radium light, wind blowing foam to fire.

Beyond storm-damage we strode a reckless sea. And you
spoke to me of Cairo, of Tahiti, Dapto, then places you
had not been, but were clearly meant to visit: 'The Gong'
where foaming carpets could unroll to lost horizons –
beyond both our aching years. Happy and heedless,
the lightning seemed to rive with smiling waste
this mundane panopticon. Out of ruined photographs of time,
bone-white, lips curled into manic arcs where faces
howled again, writhed in fiery light, strode up
from headlines. Oh could your gift again ignite these years,
our inky thumbs and pencil stubs? *Five gongs!*
Hear them! Horn, whistle! More little flashing lights!

5. Five Apples
In Melbourne, your fire became an acrid one,
your ambition too, smothered by lawn clippings,
leaves taken from a suburb's book. Smoke, but little fire
above a summer lawn, where a motor-mower spat its
divots out behind your gate. You clocked on, clocked off,
slotted merest jottings, dictated by an impulse to conform.
Briquettes kept you warm throughout the spongy winter:
persuade a drifting life of atoms, small mechanical acts,
a numbing choir of reportage, with every song the same.
Did you imagine, even then, your stake was still secure?
That you had time to wait for your number to come up, answering
fate's improbable invitation, brought to your steps on a silver plate?
Your biro (I picture it) end bitten-off, acute, harassed, could
still envenom this cosy void with a cutting line or deadly flash,
yet confessed beneath your letterhead, as I once read:
"Someone who was once living is now dead. Alas I, but a drudge

paddling shallows of that vast Harbour you still navigate as Sydney's bard. I collect my weekly cheque and pat my dog, while you ferry sheer cargo of air and light, reviving ecstasy between each quickening swell, your sails the artistry we submerge or sully with our daily living. I hear you also entertain a bit, with food and wine and wit. Hell's Bells! Forgive me this. Write soon, again. Yours, Harry."
Five Bells.

Poem for Michael Jackson:

(1958–2009)

– still counting sheep! Oh diazepan, oh man oh wham;
Oh lidocaine, I know the pain; Oh propofol don't leave me cold.
Too high to get over, too low to get under, just one tiny ring
will bring my medicine man . . . says the drip of the drip
bottle by the bed, tube to wrist, its vein thriller
chills you out, drop by drop, as unsleep's living dead falls
into a glacial all-night staring into blankness
that just stares back: the tired monkey on your back.
Bubbles the chimp frets away sleep,
you're wired with come-back nerves
rehearse ass-kick dance routines all night
slow-slip / heel-back / moonwalk freeze, turn round and shudder
endlessly awake at 3am, you're still, amazingly, Michael Jackson

turn back with the signature moves see the crowd's
excitement arc on opening night to a perfect broken leg of fame
but you're *stuck in the middle* again, with your mask of delicate
sculpted scar-tissue, Frankensteined over pale bone,
a transparent flame on the hard pillow of insomnia:
You're a vegetable, a buffet . . . body-art-piece in an all-celebrity
limited edition of one, your bleached eyes weep white.

Fall, like a trophy baby to the crowd's stunned hush . . .
No one can hurt you now . . . leave me in peace says Bubbles
who does a cute back-flip in his tiny pink tuxedo,
behind the wheel of your stretch onyx-coffin-limo,
chauffeured to endless Neverlands of fireworks, fog machines
and stardust-rainbows, to a final rocket-suit lift-off finale,
raw applause of lawyers and the coroner's itchy knife.

The industry just feasts on, its rechauffé smorgasbord,
even stone cold dead, then alleged
sly Paedo-Pan vaults were dredged,
now worth so much more
        than you ever were alive.

Business as Unusual

Metallic Shades Will Glitter Down
the Runway This Season

Headline for a fashion poster, with models dressed in
new-century guns and combat gear

A dummy's drop-dead smile best turn-prance-
strut smoke pours from reflective plumes
of fire, boneyard glitter from the fuselage,
lips and nails, our accessories so breathless . . .

Strip to glamour blasts border village strobe-path out
cross to long-armed robots   delicately snip-peck-weld
your flashy gathering of celebs   an arms industry
cashes in   ashes out your culture's cant *now!*

Throw all your casino chips at buzzy voids, metallic hues
will drone, all blown apart by black shield stealth,
electronic detection from satellites   create your own
warm delirious democratic oasis   our new fragrances
are heaven scent   *darhling!* so cashed-in so now!

It's the twisted braided look, the tied-up stress
and dog-snarl rendition of A-listers standing on one leg
off-the-rack attack of any random crowd is next
season's flash, sneak preview of the new raw war!

Bubble junk economy stupid sucks in more
bucks free fall the entire fabric cut for conflict
we got Simpsons on all fours, our new Afghani
hoods simply shriek of sheik   some guy called
the roach sub-contracts our murder take-outs, *huh!*

The laser in your grin so *now*   new bling and export
driven   so surveillance, our metallic hues will dazzle
down a burning catwalk frenzy   as factory figures
rush to Wall Street puffs a massive bubble now.

Where there's zero regulation, void's still king,
needle jets and vapour trails, tales retold of great power
exploits   overwhelming force, just imagine it, a you with
so more *you*! So *ithis*, so *ithat*! So *me-gen, so selfie now.*

Instant deaths as we recline in luxury in *haute couture*
everything we desire much *more*   overnight sensations
no degrees of separation from chip to heel to neck
will glitter down each flash of trash, that's hyper-excess now.

Cash pours liquid gold down our metallic threads
under winking satellites, re-take the retail base   night vision
goggles infra-red   the operative-designer look   guns and fur-lined
ol' glory's instant sting, eternal retro-nows.

Just watch our new season flounce its skin-deep
limbs, the anorexia shuffle, *altitudes* of attitude
walk the talk, soft power's high-to-low, inane culture's slogan sting,
a democratic DVD to peddle all our freedoms, *wow!*

Just for us   not you sucker doormat client states
consume or be consumed   so steak so sizzle so instant no-think!
so fashionably random and insincere   more gloriously rad
no reason   and if you don't salute it's treason!
metallic shades will glitter down this season's runways, *pow!*

Poems Short and Tangy

Snail, to tap-dancing centipede
What amazing feats!

More duped voters
Insulted peanuts.

Stockbroker
    One who makes you broker.

Pixel-robes
    Candles! Censers! Apps!
    Virtual Vatican on my iPope.

These things I praise
    A small flat thought,
    a lidless moment.

Critic
Everyone has one
    but not everyone is one.

Left bank
    All gave some.
    Some gave air!
    Fresh air! Plein air!
    Apollinaire!

Cover band
    Pink Fraud.

Postcard from Cuba
    Havana great time!

Locker 17

"You know, I don't talk to strangers, not usually . . .
I was on the road, I remember rain, that's all. I felt
some sort of 'kindness' reaching out . . . while driving
through towns that were so small I almost didn't see them.
This place loomed through the mist towards the hills,
long enough for me to notice its lights approaching,
the moon lit up some houses, a sign said *Welcome*.
So I stopped just near the store, behind the fork. By next
month, it's been twelve years – I've almost stopped counting.
Why am I telling you this? You asked me, I suppose.
Hey, you're good at questions. It's your job, right?
You want me to tell you, right, about . . . Locker 17?

"Marie, you ask? About her too? Well, after
our 'bold and daring crime', I landed in the slammer,
of course! Hey – we were *somebodies* back then, me and Marie!
(What did you say your name was?) Yeah, were on the news
for days. The camera crews, sirens, pictures on TV.
All that cash – in just one armoured van! That's right,
she got off lightly, barely an accomplice. I swore blind
in court she had no part in it. Because, you see, it really was
all my fault we crashed. We could have both been killed!
Never done such an ambitious job before, and really messed it up –
everything exploding! Boom! Both thrown like goldfish
from a bowl of flames, the whole road burning.
I've still got those old cuttings, down in Locker 17.

"Not long afterwards, I was in my cell, feeling pretty down,
when I read Marie's letter. '*Hope your new
"home away from home" is comfortable, old man,*'

132

was what she wrote. Marie even knew where to put the quote
marks. Educated, she never blinked at cards, so neat
with tricks. But that was years ago, just as you say.
Now I keep busy, doing things round here. Fill gas bottles,
fix locks, weld things. '*Not dead yet!*' I say that to myself each day!
Feel these scars behind my head! Go on, feel them!
As for memories! Like candles on your birthday cake:
your lips puff up, you blow, so all the flames go out.
Now just bits of drifting smoke, and Locker 17.

"Marie had slipped away, but I finally got a call,
about a year ago. We met at the motel, the one just
down the road from here. She was tense and edgy –
really not like her. She had been followed, but drove
around in circles by the lake, and shook whoever.
It was late, and we walked over to the ridge together –
such a clear and starry night! We had to talk, you see.
Marie was always straight with me. Not like the marks
and Johns. You have to trust *someone*, a special
bond. Me the same with her, both always honest
with each other. We reached the bridge, which overlooks
the lake, a full moon sobbing. I felt suspended there forever,
in that perfect moment. Could even feel her breath
against my skin! But couldn't hold it in, and blabbed –
all about my feelings. But she already knew. Always
a step ahead of me. And maybe you? So Locker 17.

"I remember what she said that night, every single word:
'*After they put you away, old man, I almost forgot
about you. I'd go for rich or poor. Didn't mind who,*

really – all just silly men, all just the same.' (She always
called me that, her 'gray old man'. Well, I just felt all gray
inside, all gray.) *'So you've held a flame, for all these years!'*
she said. *'I'm really touched, old man, but that's just how it is!
It's just too bad! I'm not* ever *going to lie to you, or sell
false hope. You know me well enough. I'll never settle down –
not now, not with you or any man! But we can still be the best
of friends, just like always.'* She kissed me on the cheek,
I dried my eyes. I knew how it would be. We talked things
through, we made some plans . . . and Locker 17.

"Look at that, it's getting late! I still don't know why
I'm telling you all this, about my life! I suppose just to
get things off my chest. Next day, she waved goodbye.
I haven't seen her since. Hey mister, so you already *know*
about all this? But not about her things down there?
Only some old papers, hats, white gloves, a perfumed scarf
Marie would wear. *'Please keep them safe for me,'* she said.
Oh yeah, and a letter too, that someone might collect one day;
but it could take years, or never. Now that I see you better,
in this light, you're exactly as she said. So, you're the lucky one,
heh? Everything is exactly as she left it, in Locker 17.

"You know, I almost see her sometimes; when the wind
plays tricks. I'd do anything for her. The door is taped to keep
the rattles quiet. There's some stairs; a skylight way above you
in the roof. And when you pass the smashed-in floor, be careful.
Don't look up at it. No, I never did read that letter,
as I said, it wasn't meant for me. Sometimes I take her
perfumed scarf out. Just to look, hold close, and remember her.

We kissed, and she told me what to do. I sobbed to watch
her leave. I can't tell you any more, about her, or true love,
or *anything*. (I'll stay close behind you, with my torch.)
Yes, *this* key! On your way down now, to Locker 17!"

Slow Dissolve for Mr. D.

He edged his sickle closer, spreading shaving foam
below his nose, enough to soften the black wires
poking from his upper lip. There was no reflection
in the mirror, and would never be. He must imagine
his own face floating somewhere in his mind,
then place it on the surface of the glass. His eyes were
sackcloth and declined both light and flesh, to parody
the qualms of human kind. And the most enduring
nightmare, a likeness of Black Death. *Beware, Mortals,*
of what you dream . . . I am your dream. He tilted back
his hood a little, just to angle down the blade, despatching
bristles quickly, and sent them spinning in the sink. *"Abra Cadabra,*
Cadaver!" He intoned. Then patted dry his shaven face.

Mr. D. splashed reeking after-shave from a polished phial,
regarding curiously the pair of sneakers that had appeared
below his gown a few days before. Perhaps there was
a need to seem more cheerful? For a moment, he missed
his old black clogs, and frowned. But smile or glower
were both dreadful on his face, and had equally erased
the halting glance of many a supplicant or last-breath-taker.
Still, a flicker of amity had replaced the usual grim mask –
some presage, perhaps, that men and women might
be about to turn in their collective sleep and clothe him
in a newly renovated apprehension of their dread:
Medieval harvest garb in tatters, begrimed with dust and ash,
the pooled image of their tears, their useless fears.

His black-rimmed 'shades' were a recent touch, erasing
something darker, veiling his vast sockets. But what a party trick!

to whip them off at the dramatic moment, yell 'Gotcha Dude!'
or some such catchphrase! He put the cap back on the fragrant
bottle: *"Paint an inch thick, when to this favour all must come?"*
On his iPad, Mr. D. Googled 'Population Clock': today, seven
and a quarter billion lives! Shaking his head at how humanity
had doubled, or just about, since 1965. Each new birth a death,
a sand grain pouring. He tipped his hourglass back and saw,
in that single minute, more than a hundred lives were gone.
"Give or take a few – but mainly take!" Then called he roughly
his invisibles about him! His swarms of reapers – the doubles
of himself, the effigies, the multiples and avatars – were infinite.

Mr. D. walked down Regent Street, and sat upon a bench,
dejected, wept with head in hands. It was no good to pretend,
he felt sick unto death with all the teeming forfeiture of Earth.
He spread his trailing gown around him, a silken sea of onyx.
What sort of pale occupation his, fated to attend, day after day,
the last man or woman standing, until time's end! While dumb
happiness was commonplace to all the passers-by before him,
on the street and still undone. But there was consolation
in his reaping stroke, and follow-through, both true as steel.
His blade was nonpareil, whispering its severe refreshment like
an icy kiss. How to explain, and make them see his work was just . . .
life? You have already won at cosmic chance! So be resigned!
To be at all . . . *was* all! 'Just doin' my job, Man. I got no axe to grind!'

Was he in fashion? Was he out? As he entered the emporium, Mr. D.
turned straight to menswear, he'd soon learn: sleeved down to the waist,
velvet sash and cape, a huge black pointy hood, dark glasses
and wan face, the 'cobwebby' look. The nice salesgirl apprised

him, "Retro Goth! So cool!" and snatched some rags 'n things
for him to wear. "*The Addams Family* look doesn't suit you, sir,
someone with your smile," she cajoled expertly. "Black was
the new black last year, now it's harlequin and collars." "Yeh,
but dead's the same old dead!" he guffawed, and tried a velvet tie,
a turquoise cape, a crimson belt, some clean white gloves.
"Sir cuts quite a dash," she said, as he stood and peered before
a vacant full-length mirror. "Now," he demanded, "something for
the beach!" She rubbed her eyes. "Yes, certainly! Come this way, sir."

As he sauntered through, with old Trusty Rusty by his side, the X-Ray
at the boarding queue spiked off the graph. "You will have to check
        your . . .
utensil . . . into stowage, sir – we don't take sharps on board!"
Stretched out later in his window seat, he watched the Classic Movie
Channel, Bergman's *Seventh Seal*. Again, the knight had missed
the perfect chance to cheat him. No rule against deferring moves –
for centuries perhaps. Checkmate, so good (k)night! They flew
towards the sun, and he found his appetite. He turned the air vents
overhead – he never felt the cold – and wolfed down in-flight meals.
He turned his headset on, 'chilled out' to arctic ice, until he tired
and snored. A flight attendant saw one bony knee protrude, kindly
placing blankets for him, and thereby – though she didn't know it –
earned, for her own finalé, the kindest possible "Lights out, sir?"

He was met at the airport by a shuttle bus. "Sorry I'm late,
Bud," said the driver. "Don't be – I'm used to it!" joked the tall
dark figure, now in Hawaiian shirt and beach shorts: when,
for one brief tick in time, the world was free of loss. "Honolulu
is sure a lulu of a place!" "Yep, sure is! I got you down for

Waikiki, sir!" the driver said. "That's right." The air was
clement, trade winds bending palms, as they sped down Queen
Liliuokalani Highway, with old Slicer hanging out the window.
He was excited like a kid. Was this what they called happiness?
As poet John Donne had said, *"Death, thou shalt die . . . "* Or, if not
decease, at least desist and call a kindly halt. Perhaps two weeks?
Then recalled to mind how he'd given Donne a good eye-popping
Manifestation for such flippant lines. No more same old slash
    and grind!

The Aloha Beach Resort was new and well-appointed. He rose
early for a swim; hanging by the pool all afternoon. A lively crew
were playing on the sand, and threw a beach ball up to him.
He said "hi" to all the faces gathered round, agreeing
to meet later at the bar, the Tiki, and watch a tennis match.
He'd pretty soon made friends with a friendly guy called Boris,
a former KGB spy, turned share-trader in the new Russia.
Old 'Lights Out' liked Russians, the hammer and sickle
an attractive icon. And Boris had already paired with Benny,
an insurance broker from NZ, and Benny's girlfriend, Bunny,
who'd shovelled Himalayan servings for him, toppling on a plate.
"You gotta fatten up now," Bunny shrieked. "Grow love handles,
just like me! Looky, Mr. Skin and Bones! Eat up, try a steak!"

He forked more cold cuts down, as Benny laughed and slapped him
on the back! "Hey, here's Boris and the girls! Let's have fun!"
(*Mr. D. still picturing the swollen liver that would one day
bring poor Benny low. But that was years off, with many
good years still to go . . .*) as they caroused again poolside, sampled
triple Zombies, mixing Mai Tais complete with nodding

frangipanis as they talked. "Me? Name's Mortimer D. Ceased,"
he lugubriously intoned to them. His nifty business card was
  coffin-shaped.
"I'm in the funerals game!" he perked. Benny and the others shook
his hand. "Nice card. But, no disrespect, Pal, that's a real
'down' occupation that you got. Ever thought of changing it?"
"Old family trade," he said. "With huge demand! It's really quite
a sunny job. Hey – I do discounts! And you can call me Mortie!"
They laughed. "Great to meet you, Mortie! Let's hit the sand!"

He joined the 'Fabulous Frisbee Flingers', a corny bunch
of sand habitués. "There's a party on tomorrow – in costumes,"
Boris yelled. "With prizes for best dressed! I'm going to go as Zorro!"
A radio played somewhere, air full of slide guitars, but broken
by the local news, about a puzzling, " . . . *world-wide decline in
  mort . . .* "
And riffling through the papers, Mr. D. noted cartoons had replaced
obituaries that day . . . When, suddenly, he felt a sort of 'far away'
sensation, as his entire left hand, without the slightest warning,
disappeared before his eyes. His arm began to follow it, sucked into
an instant void. He blinked, and there it was again, as usual. Phew!
No punters for a week or more, so fear was ebbing from the world.
The fantasy that sustained him was dissolving. Unpack his mothballed
Robe, his rusting Blade, whetstone . . . ! He grasped at once what he
  must do.

Bunny looked a very raffish Pirate at the annual Waikiki costume party
that balmy, starry evening. Earlier, Mr. D. had dusted off his
  old ensemble.
Downstairs, everyone was already jumping to the band, delirious

in a centrifuge of happy faces melting past. Mort felt his pulse leap,
and conga'd over with the others, then triple-somersaulted
through the air, slicing all the wooden legs from an empty chair
on his way down. "Look at that!" "Go, Mortie!" Drum roll and a crash!
The MC took the floor: "Give it up for . . . Bunny, in second place!"
Another crash and thump! "First prize to . . . The Reaper! The
      man noone
ever beats!" The band's lead singer draped a double lathe of flowers
over him. He kissed her lips, which made her head spin. "Wow!"
      She staggered
back and nearly fainted. "Thank you everyone! Now, let's dance!
      Let's party!
Dance now, for your lives!" "*If we took a holiday . . . it would be so
nice . . .*"

It was about four a.m. when Mortie, still in festive garlands,
strolled arm in arm along the gentle beach with dancer Cherry,
both still tipsy, but elated, without a seeming trouble in the world.
"Old Son," she said. "To happiness! Just let the good times roll, heh!"
They agreed to meet, "Same time, same place!" again next year.
Mr. D. could see, beyond her smile, his female counterpart:
"Fancy meeting *you* here!" She just hummed a little tune
in her smoky alto, Gounod's *Funeral March of a Marionette*!
"Hey – we have the same great taste in music!" The fragrant reef
fell hushed, the stars arched overhead. He said good night, as both now
had to fly. Two little figures wavered in the fickle light, with fading
purchase on the air, and soon goodbye. *There*, and then *not there*!
Soon, above the beach of Waikiki, was just a pale sickle moon.

He floated in his golden robe above the clouds, high in a dream
he'd seldom known before, so light and elevating: tender as a falling
flower, his true shape now revealed, began a rain of blossom over
all the oceans, falling like the tears of those who ever mourned. He took
the form of Thanatos, twin to Hypnos, he of gentle sleep.
Then of Raindrop, then of warming light upon a wall. He could be
however they imagined him to be, for he was nothing at all.
He heard a wailing on the wind, of those whose time had come,
attentive to the desperate ones, who cried for his return, the sick,
the frail and suffering whose pain he could not spurn or selfishly
postpone. He, whose touch was peace now, their release the sweetest
blessing, could not refuse his love! Threw back his head and cackled
high, assumed his hood and blade again. Then spread his cape
    and flew.

Trance Formations

The Annual Eros Motor Joyride

Ladies and gentlemen, or whoever, start your engines!
We're turbo-charged and edgy, our silver duco
flashing sunlight – all engines purr, ignitions on:
tossed in the air, jocks and frilly panties floating
everywhere, as we take off, spinning into place
in our sparkling *'Libido Convertible Sedan'.*
Sprinting down fair motorways of *Eros.*
        ('Libido Sedan'. A popular domestic roadster,
        fully reversible seating, with mirrored roof.)

Beside the road, a huge depiction of Herr Freud,
reclining in his *'Vintage Couch',* with its down upholstery
and small brass coasters. Then flat-out on the raceway strip
the 'Siggy Sighway', we zoom beneath his legs,
deft slips of tongue, as engines grunt and growl!
        (The 'Vintage Couch'. Also runs on rail lines,
        from the Talking Cure company.)

My co-driver, curled up close, slips between me
and the wheel. Balanced on the steering column,
we shimmy clothes away, now naked flesh to flesh –
take each turn with ease: a skid, a screech, hold on! –
shocks of surprised delight, as we both come at once.
Drive on harder – we thrill a corner on two wheels,
and dart away: *white lines white lines white lines!*

A nifty *'Kama Sutra Hatch'* ahead. Its expert yogi crew,
while intoning *Ommm,* flip through the Karmic manual:
'Lingam of the Bird' in overdrive; such exotic skills!
'Congress of the Locust', 'Persimmon and Honey Yoni'.

Their *Hatch* stops and turns. In our rear-view, see them
perform 'Congress of the Black Bee', while driving in reverse!
('Kama Sutra Hatch'. With fold-out drinks tray, and optional
collapsible spa complete with floating petals.)

Our '*Libido*' overtakes a slinky '*Coitus Roadster*' next,
then leather-lined '*Erotes Coupé*', so-named after the wingéd
demi-gods of Aphrodite's troupe. Heh! – the sky opens, pouring
rain, with an erotic lightning flash, as fogged-up
windscreens blur with mist – and off again we dash.
('Coitus Roadster'. A self-lubricating vehicle, fully solar, producing
zero emissions. Won the prestigious 'Green Wet Dream Award'.)

A nippy '*Lesbos Sport*', with breathtaking silky speed,
escorts a sleek '*Gaycloud Sedan*', both number-plated *LGBTI*.
Never out of style, they glide the road together, such a happy peloton
of thrust and pleasure. We see the '*Gaycloud*', front and rear drive,
throw hard right, become a blur of purring pink and white.
('Lesbos Sport'. Electronic fold-out wings, huge range of
upholstery, from work denim to pure silk.)

Flat to the floor: more juice, more juice, we're cruising on!
She grabs the wheel from me, and throws our sleek '*Libido*'
down a seaside strip, where fetishists draped in tiny furs,
voyeurs with lorgnettes held high, cheer us from the roadside.
We blow kisses back, and double on the gas – when . . .
Wham! Bham! A pulsating thump-mobile '*Auto-Erotic*',
full of rapping P-plate Onanists, tail-gates from behind.
('Auto Erotic'. The ever popular alternative,
with great road handling.)

A brand-new 'Percy Panel Van', now in cruise control,
fills the lane beside us, upholstered in *faux* dingo-hide,
with doonas and frangers, every amenity supplied, plus beer taps
in the ample 'bedroom', gives its Oz crew a sporting ride!
　　(Percy Panel Van, with roof surfboard rack
　　and roller blinds.)

A silky 'Perfumed Garden' overtakes, to lead the way ahead,
ducoed in *au naturale* flesh-tones. Promoted as 'an exotic delirium
on wheels', it's one-eyed driver Mr. Al Dekhal, playfully prods
his passenger, she with the little nose, Ms Ella Moudd.
　　(The classic 'Perfumed Garden'. Complete with
　　console scent ducts and floral décor.)

A 'Thrust Convertible' whispers into view;
full of 'someone I just met at the office, dear'
and 'don't worry, we're just good friends' – all frantically
getting much friendlier; negotiates another curve.
　　(The reliable 'Thrust Convertible';
　　of Irish manufacture, licence plate FECK.)

Into condemnatory *Thanatos* we roll, our major test – that nightmare,
po-faced place, provokes a haze of fluoro danger flags:
more dead ends, road-blocks, black-ice bends! We stay behind
a grinding 'Root-Ute All-Terrain' to avoid the smoking wreckage.
Dire Thanatos is lined with burnt-out hulks and random carnage.
At last, we exit through a slip lane! Phew! We speed on!
　　(The 'Root-Ute All-Terrain'. Promoted as 'no road
　　too bumpy', ideal for Outback touring.)

We safely fly the course as evening falls
and stars appear; ahead the chequered flag!
As dawn climbs into view, sweet strips of bunting fly.
Our neat *'Libido'* escorts a looming *'Coitus Roadster'*,
the *'Gaycloud'* next, then *'Lesbos'* followed by a
'Stretch Libido Max'. Another and another . . .
and another hits the finish line, all bright
and streaming bullets down life's highway!

It's just the human race, and how we got here:
"Planet Earth, Population, 7 billion and a bit,"
says a flashing roadside sign. The drivers
and the driven, all elated, catch their breath.

Oh, how we trailed our raunchy smoke –
a delirium of acrid love, nearly barbecued our tyres,
sparks from our wheels divine, down life's delicious highway.
Coitus at last, our spasms spun, sweet climax won!

Now cool down and catch our breath
at last. But wait – one vehicle still dawdles,
barely halfway home. A *'Stretch-Delayed-Climax-Ultimate-Defer'*
stops endlessly along the way for fore- and after-play.
"So we're slow. We know, so what. What flag?
What finish line? Who cares?!"
> *(The 'Stretch-Delayed-Climax-Ultimate-Defer'*
> *luxury vehicle. Company motto: 'Linger longer –*
> *your life-affirming holiday on wheels.')*

When He Read the Poem in the Room Above the Stairs

1.
When he read the poem in the room above the stairs,
the walls had been repainted, and a new skylight put in.
He approached from the lane, a mirror near the steps,
and when he glanced, had hardly recognised himself.
As he looked to see that his pages were in order,
he noticed old photographs of people – older poets
he had once known – had been removed,
and a glass-topped bench with new vases on it.
As he began to read, the poem stayed
exactly the same as always, not a comma or character
or pause had ever been replaced. And as his voice
rose to meet it, he realised how little ever changed.
He was still himself, for better or worse. As always,
the audience sat courteously, still listening, and fragile.
Whether full or empty, the room was just a room.

2.
When he read the poem in the room above the stairs,
he imagined it was full of blind people, and it was hard
to read their expressions. So many dark glasses, black
as the shiny coffee served here. He rubbed his eyes,
he knew he'd have to discard the poem he once thought balanced
and complete, and continued in a brave, quiet panic.
At which point the room filled with light, and dazzled
off the walls and lit up cups. It shot sharp lances
from the sides of things, so intense it made his eyes well
with tears. He thanked the room, which had shrunk in the glare
to the size of a pinhole. Putting the thought away, he smiled.

3.
When he read the poem in the room above the stairs,
people felt they could hear things they had forgotten.
As he read, and they listened, his voice reached out
across the space, or was suspended in the air. Beyond
the room, he remembered wind and rain, sighs shot through
with longing, sounds climbing like some impossibly high staircase
of emotion, that was not his and seemed to belong to no one.
The audience, in contrast, heard sounds of journeys never made.
As he read, all these things could slip away, back into silence,
they were accounted for, and finally done – and the poem returned
to absence where words had been, a listening without regret.
So he raised his voice, and looked down where a girl
was doodling the word *more* in a cold winter's morning.
But it was summer now, and the room flashed past, shuddering,
as if at speed, merging into other words not yet written.
He read until the poem was entirely given away. At the end
of this, he knew it was not raining outside, and could not be.
He would always be in this room. Had always been, forever.
Beside him, another self sat and wondered. At last, he sipped
his coffee, sailed out, still listening carefully. Below the stairs,
out in the air, found the marvellous street and sun.

Parable of the Lobster and the Brick

There are many stories about piano-playing lobsters,
about lobsters in late-night bars, on the concert
platform, lobsters travelling on subways, and so on,
and I suppose you have heard quite of a few them,
have even collected autographs or shaken hands
with some famous examples . . . But the only lobster
that I ever knew well, or with any degree of intimacy,
played a small metal piano of the type given to
children, the sort with blue and white notes,
that are sometimes found discarded in attics. Although, he
did play it exceptionally well . . . And there was no bar
in this lobster's story – well, not until the story's end –
because he did like an occasional drink, just as
anyone does . . . Anyway, this lobster wore a soft, ruffed,
red-velvet suit with braces and a sort of little bib pulled
up over the hard, red-enamel panels of his outer shell –
I mean the shell that was actually part of him,
and not a stage costume – and he had hundreds of little
sparkling diamantes on the ends of his feelers and claws
that lit up in the bright stage lights, all accentuated
with a diamond tie-pin. This created an interesting
theatrical effect, one never lost on an audience.
He would swivel around slowly on the piano stool
and with a big, cheesy smile, say: "*I am soooo
glaaad that you have come heeeere tonight . . . !*"

The lobster also did some impressions and funny voices,
or told a few jokes, as part of his warm-up act,
and on this particular night, he sang Italian opera highlights,
and little bits of mock opera, which sounded like

the real thing but were really invented on the spot.
I suppose this amused him and was also part
of the generosity he felt towards his audience.
Well, who knows what goes through a lobster's mind
in such a moment ..? It's just you, up there on stage,
with the lights in your eyes, and your feelers full of diamantes.

This night, he began working with the Italian word for cheese,
which is 'formaggio', or 'platto di formaggio',
which is a garbled 'plate of cheese', singing in mock-operatic style:
"Platto! di! formaggio! forma-forma-mag-gi-o!
Platto! di! formaggio!" And sometimes he would
also do some very basic and, I suppose, quite silly
impressions, such as becoming a willow tree . . .
Tonight, he stood in front of the audience with his feelers
and long spiky legs and claws all swaying, slowly from side
to side, while making sound-effects – *"Ssshhhh ssshhhhhh . . ."*
which was the sound of the wind whooshing through the leaves,
as he swayed . . . Anyway, you probably guessed it . . . on this
particular night, there was an obnoxious drunk in the audience,
who rose from his chair and shouted: *"I came here for some serious*
music, not a lobster doing an impression of a fucking willow tree!"

The lobster was not fazed, but just sat down and teased
a long, twinkling arpeggio from the keyboard – *dinga dinga*
dinga ding – then looked slowly over his left feeler, with a very
quizzical stalked eye, at the drunk – which was actually
a signal to the bouncer, who took the drunk outside
and beat him up a little, until he was in an appropriately
receptive mood for great art, and then sat the fellow back

down in his seat. Meanwhile, by that time, the lobster
was playing a Chopin étude, with great concentration
and sensitivity, just as the spotlight narrowed to an intense
beam, highlighting the lobster's face and rapt
expression, in a bright pool above the keyboard.

Actually, when not on stage, the lobster lived mainly
on the Sandringham tram, in scraps of dishevelled newspaper
pulled over his claws, like something left over from a prawn
and beer night. That's how, he said, he found his inspiration.
He lived that way by choice, not out of necessity,
and would travel back and forth, from Sandringham to the city,
forth and back, without sometimes saying a single word.
His companion at these times was a red wire-cut
house brick: his constant companion, really.
And the two would travel together, side by side,
on the seat of the tram – the lobster in his bits of
newspaper, and the brick just sitting there, on the seat.

The two had lots of things in common, they were both
red, approximately the same size, and both did
impressions – except that the brick was more regular
and geometric in shape and, of course, much heavier.
The brick, actually, did only *one* impression . . .
He did an impression of a house brick. That is,
he did an impression of *himself*, as a brick.
The lobster thought his friend amazingly 'deep',
a real artist whom not everyone 'got' straight away.
The lobster would nudge other passengers and say:
"Look at that brick – he's doing himself again."

Anyway, it was amazing to find these two together,
there was such a bond and accord between them,
such true regard and politeness. You don't often
see that any more. For example, when they alighted
from their tram, the lobster would hold back, and say,
"Oh, you first." And the brick would say, *"I wouldn't dream
of it . . . after you, I'm sure."* And the lobster would
gesture with a flourish, *"No, no, my very good friend,
I insist, after you!"* And if they were at a restaurant,
and arrived at the same time, the lobster would
pull back the brick's seat with some considerable style,
and say, *"Dear Monsieur Brick, Mon Ami, please be seated –
as my guest."* And the brick would say, *"No, but you are
too kind. Of course, you must be seated first, Monsieur
Lobster. And, of course, naturally, you are* my *guest."*

And so on. Well, this night, the lobster worked his magic at
the keyboard, and with such close attention, his feelers
began to quiver and sway as he played. Even the drunk
had calmed down and was now ecstatic. And although the lobster
was playing very well, and the audience were already under
his spell, he stopped abruptly and inquired, very softly
and with great gentleness, addressing the front row: *"Is there
a Beryl in the audience?"* The lobster heard a short intake
of breath – of surprise, perhaps – as a hand rose slowly.

"Beryl," said the lobster, *"I have a message . . . from Alf.
He says that you should stop grieving, because time is an illusion
in eternity – and he hasn't really left you. Alf says he wants
you to sell the ring and find happiness. That is your true purpose in life."*

The woman stifled a sob and slight faint, "*Thank you so, so much.*"
The lobster continued playing his Chopin . . . Again, his feelers trembled
as the effortless, plangent notes lifted and fell from his lightning
skitterings across the keyboard. Again, the lobster stopped abruptly.
"*A message from . . . From . . . coming through now, for Martha!
Is Martha here?*" A shy hand rose, from a back row. "*It's from . . . Fritz!*"

The lobster swayed a little, adjusted his feelers, then said:
"*Fritz says, he forgives you and forgives himself. He says,
'If you could only see the stars pouring in from . . . 'the place' . . . but it's
far away now. He will see you again, but you must learn to 'let go'
and be happy, for now.*" The lobster liked to convey these messages
from '*the other side*', even if it meant interrupting his playing. (Well,
he had these talents . . .) This night, however, although he didn't know
    it,
his friend, the brick, was in the audience, and suddenly, and to his
enormous surprise, a message for the brick came through.
"*Is the brick really here?*" he asked. "*Yes, indeed, kind sir.*"
The brick certainly was – sitting, with a new bow tie, in the third row.
"*Brick,*" he said, "*I will tell you later,*" and went back to his playing.

It was well after the last notes and applause had died,
and after he had taken his final bow, that the lobster left
the concert hall and met the brick. (At a bar, as it turned
out.) The two sipped their martinis slowly, while the lobster
told his friend what he had picked up from the either.
"*Or is that ether?*" he asked. "*Either,*" said the brick. I will condense
the story, as it's getting late. Besides, the ruddy duo want
to catch their tram back to Sandringham. Well, it seems the clay
from which the brick was made (as the lobster explained) was

actually of the kind used for making house tiles, *not* bricks. *"For tiles, not bricks!"* You see, fate had intended the brick to be a tile, not a brick. On the day the brick was made, the *wrong* clay had arrived at the brickworks, but nobody had noticed. Very carefully, the lobster broke this to his friend.

The brick actually took the news quite well. *"Ah,"* he said he had often *"wondered . . . "* Perhaps even *"suspected, as much"*. At which, the lobster was quick to remind him – of the great *similarities*. Were not bricks and tiles equally important, both excellent insulators, impervious to bright sunshine and any sort of weather? And he, the brick, after all, was surely not alone. There were many others in the same batch. And so on . . .

Yes, the brick not only took it fairly well, but continued to do his single impression – of himself just being a brick, one who was intended to be a clay tile but, after all, was now a brick. The brick became a philosopher of sorts. *"Tile by clay, brick by name,"* but always, *"brick by nature!"*

And the lobster? Well, the lobster, more and more, trusted less and less in first impressions . . . And was always prepared to be surprised by life, and by people, too – and to accept them exactly as they were, as nothing more or less than the particular outcome of their own peculiar histories. And he knew that everyone had a story to tell. And he never tired of telling them, to himself and to the hushed faces beyond his twinkling keyboard. And on his tram, in his crumpled paper cape, he never tired of being amazed.

Poems Short and (Almost) Silent

Davina's dream
I float through those white rooms
above the white piano –
see something is moving,
everything hovers there,
don't touch the keys!
The music plays itself.

Early Winter
On the darkest ridge line
the road dips and turns away,
an old gate hangs from nothing,
clouds and seasons race:
air sighs up there –
chill stars flicker, bits of moon,
where another post is leaning.
Hardly a word spoken, inside or out,
no work done today, nothing achieved.
Fence wires sift the wind.

Nature held in light sleep
Your being here,
a side-effect of breathing,
    our trace floats on air,
the sky inside us:
ardent shade, winter sun.

Overheard, after rain
    "Smell the quiet!"

Rock, scissors, paper . . .
    Paper! – ok then,
    it's a wrap!

About the Author

John Jenkins has been writing poetry since 1967, and is the author of nine collections. He also writes non-fiction, short stories, radio plays and sometimes for live performance. Born in Melbourne in 1949, John lived in Sydney in the 1970s, and has worked extensively as a journalist, both at home and overseas. He more recently taught in colleges and universities, but now writes full-time. John won the 2003 Arts Rush/Shoalhaven Poetry Prize; 2004 James Joyce Suspended Sentence Award; 2013 Melbourne Poets Union International Poetry Prize and 2018 Ellyn Mitchell Short Story Award. He has presented master classes in Dublin and Singapore. John lives near Victoria's Yarra Valley, on the semi-rural fringes of Melbourne. He enjoys walking, good wine and hopes for a better world.

Notes on the Poems

Meyer Lansky's shady dealings in Havana have been comprehensively documented by the Cuban writer Enrique Cerules, and I am indebted to him for my initial imagining of Lansky in *Under the Shaded Blossom.* In the poem, 'Big Lucky' refers to Lucky Luciano, Lansky's boss and head of the Sicilian Mafia in New York; while 'Mr. Stevens' is based on the great American poet and unlikely insurance executive, Wallace Stevens, who first visited Havana in 1923. Stevens travelled frequently to Florida and Miami, and may have dined in places that gangsters later frequented. Importantly, my two characters are based on real people, but are essentially fictional, as is their unlikely meeting. The point is that sinister slickers like Lansky often rubbed shoulders – in the casinos and playgrounds of bad old Havana – with highly respectable tourist businessmen such as Stevens. Some fragments and echoes of poems by Wallace Stevens (jumbled with other thoughts and printed in italics) are made to become part of the poet's daydreams and musings. In his letters, Stevens tells us that Cuba reminded him of certain brine-scented scenes in *The Tempest*, and echoes of Shakespeare's play shade into Stevens' interior monologues.

Puissance is written in memory of the great German equestrian, Dr. Reiner Klimke (1936–1999) who excelled in the Olympics from 1960 to 1988. Klimke followed the true classical method, and employed highly ethical and non-cruel training, insisting that the horse should enjoy its work, and be one with the rider. *Hohe Schule; haute école cheval* (German; French; 'the highest school', of dressage). *Bascule, piaffe, capriole, courbette, airs above the ground, pirouette* (specific dressage movements). *Sturm-pferde* (German, 'storm-horse').

Henri Matisse, Spring Studio, Nice. The poem refers to the Matisse painting, *'Reclining Nude. The Painter and his Model 1935'.* Matisse first went to Paris to study law, but later discovered in art, "a kind of paradise". Re *doves*: there is a famous photograph by Henri Cartier-Bresson of Henri Matisse in his Nice studio on the French Riviera, surrounded by pet doves. *Amélie* was Matisse's second wife, and also his model. The poem also refers to an earlier Matisse painting, *'Luxe, Calme et Volupté'* (Luxury, Peace and Pleasure) after a poem by Charles Baudelaire.

The Traveller (Man with a Suitcase) while not being strictly ekphrastic, is certainly a very appreciative nod to Australian painter Jeffrey Smart's *The Traveller 1973.*

Coathanger, the Opera tells the sweeping saga of the Sydney Harbour Bridge, and contains brief quotes from historians, participants and witnesses. The songs (in italics) are my own poor invention, as is the dramatic fiction/conceit of an opera being written and composed, on the run as it were, as the poem unfolds.

Maxwell's Field. Einstein said that " . . . relativity owes its origins to Maxwell's equations." Scientist, mathematician and poet James Clerk Maxwell predicted the existence of electromagnetic waves, later experimentally verified. In addition, their predicted speed was the same as the measured speed of light, proving that light is also an electromagnetic wave. In many ways, Maxwell pioneered a new understanding of physical reality, and his 'field equations' arguably underpin our new 'digital age', including its devices and inventions.

Birdsong Far Away was written after *Undue Voice: Tremor*, a hybrid poetry/music performance in which I participated, staged at The Performance Space, Castlemaine, as part of the 2009 Melbourne Writers Festival, which featured electronic musicians James Hullick (from the *Buggatronics* ensemble) and visiting virtuoso Swiss percussionist Daniel Beuss.

Hanuman Society. Hanuman is the Hindu monkey god; here commenting on human evolution and ethics. The poem's title is a pun on 'Human Society'.

The Tent at Evening contains two italicised quotes: one from 'Midnight Train to Georgia', a classic soul/funk song by Gladys Knight and the Pips, and another from *'Largo al Factotum',* from Rossini's opera, *The Barber of Seville.*

Charles Dodgson in Cheshire. Lewis Carroll's actual name was Charles Lutwidge Dodgson (1832–1898) and the first draft of this poem was written on Carroll's birthday, January 27. Of course, John Milton (1608–1674) who is also mentioned, wrote the breath-takingly serious *Paradise Lost.* The poem contains two italicised quotes: *dreaming spires* is from Matthew Arnold, and the three quoted lines of poetry are from *'Poéme du Chat'* (Poem of the Cat), by Claude-Antoine Guyot-Desherbiers (my translation).

Michael as a Glider Plane was written in the 'heroic psychedelic' style of the early 1970s. It contains an (italicised) quote from Ken Taylor's poem, 'Autumn Drunk', and another from Alison Hill's 'Observations'. It is a homage to a wonderful friend to many, Michael Dugan.

Hell's Bells. This frayed and disreputable poem is a cheeky homage (disguised as semi-parody) obviously mirroring the style and structure of Kenneth Slessor's magnificent poem, *Five Bells*. I ask the forgiveness of anyone who feels I have taken too many liberties here, as I have unbounded admiration for Slessor's original. Imitation being the sincerest form of . . . etc.

Poem for Michael Jackson has italicised quotes from his song, 'Wanna be Startin' Somethin''.

Slow Dissolve for Mr. D. has three italicised quotes; the first from Shakespeare's *Hamlet;* the second from John Donne, *Death be not proud,* and third from a Madonna song, 'Holiday'.

Parable of the Lobster and the Brick. This poem was transcribed from a dream immediately upon waking, word for word, with very little alteration. The Lobster seems a little like Liberace, and the entire poem an elaborate, cartoon-like joke.

Acknowledgements

The following have variously been placed, short-listed, or have won Australian poetry competitions: *Under the Shaded Blossom; When He Read the Poem in the Room Above the Stairs; Kelly at the Mines; The Traveller (Man with a Suitcase); The Rabbit-Proof Sonnet; Freeway, Flyover, and Back; Henri Matisse, Spring Studio, Nice; Domino and Tabby; Maxwell's Field; The Wedgetails; Charles Dodgson in Cheshire; The Tent at Evening; Hell's Bells; Slow Dissolve for Mr. D.*

Individual poems have been previously published in *Ultra-Short Poems, Coolabah Journal*, Barcelona, Spain, 2018; *Suburban Whistlestop, Poets @ Watsonia*, Melbourne Poets Union, 2018; *Connective Tissue*, Newcastle Poetry Prize (NPP) Anthology, 2015; *Australian Poetry Members Anthology*, 2014; *Once Wild,* NPP Anthology, 2014; *Stillcraic* online poetry, 2014; *Memory Weaving*, Poetica Christi Press, 2014; *Now You Shall Know*, NPP Anthology, 2013; *Island Magazine*, 2013; *Australian Love Poems*, Inkerman & Blunt, 2013; *Poetry Reach* online,

Ireland, 2013; 'Perambulations', episode of ABC Radio National's Poetica, 2013; *Writers Radio*, Radio Adelaide, 2013; *Coastline*, NPP Anthology, 2012; *The Best Australian Poems*, Black Inc, 2012; *Divan online*, 2012; *Gesher Magazine*, 2012; *The Best Australian Poems*, Black Inc, 2011; *Contemporary Australian Poetry* (in translation) Australia–China Council, 2007; *The Honey Fills the Cone*, NPP Anthology, 2006; *The Best Australian Poems*, Black Inc, 2006; *Blue Dog Magazine*, 2006; *The Best Australian Poems*, Black Inc, 2005; *Melbourne Poets Union Newsletter*, 2006; *Heat Magazine*, 2005; *Cordite Poetry Review online*, 2005; *Artstreams Magazine*, 2005; *The Plot Thickens: Narratives in Australian Art*, exhibition, Heide Gallery, 2004; *Overland Magazine*, 2001; *Readings Bookshop*, 1995; *Hobo Magazine*, 1994; *Salt Magazine*, 1990.

Many thanks to all concerned at P&W, and to helpful friends who gave insightful feedback on this book and made valuable suggestions.

www.ingramcontent.com/pod-product-compliance
Lightning Source LLC
Chambersburg PA
CBHW030835090426

42737CB00009B/979